STEFANO ZARDINI

CORTINA

LIGHT ®
HUNTER

INDICE

THE ORIGINS,   when the Dolomites were the sea bed...   6

THE LANDSCAPE, among rocks, wood and silences, to be discovered on foot.   20

THE HISTORY,   fascinating and unique for over 1000 years.   44

THE VISITORS,   from the early Englishmen of the past century to current tourism. 62

THE TRADITIONS, so ancient and rooted in their wholeness.   78

THE SNOW,   the season during which Cortina changes.   102

LIGHT HUNTER PUBLICATIONS

Stefano Zardini
via Jacheto 10
32043 CORTINA
(Belluno) ITALY
Tel. 0436 · 2930
Fax 0436 · 868342

POTOGRAPHS BY
Stefano Zardini

GRAPHIC DESIGN
M.T. Mezzacappa
TEXTS BY
Maria Cristina Todeschini
Silvia Datei

PRINTING

Plants:
Sartori · Treviso
Composition:
Aquarello · Pieve di C. (BL)
Printing:
GMV · Villorba/Treviso
Distributor:
Light Hunter Publications
Cortina

© by
LIGHT HUNTER PUBLICATIONS
32043 CORTINA ITALY

REPRODUCTION

THE ORIGINS

WHEN THE DOLOMITES WERE THE SEA BED...

"...Looking around in all directions the Prince then saw that on every peak, in the entire realm, a bright spot was burning; on every peak the dwarfs had woven the moonrays. It was as if the stars in the sky had come down to rest on the peaks of the dark mountains. The next morning, the valley-dwellers could not believe what they saw: the mountains that the day before had risen so dark towards the sky, now seemed to have grown dim. In only one night, the small Salvani had managed to dress all the mountains in the realm with the bright light of the moon regions." (C. F. Wolf, I monti pallidi, 1913).

The history of the Dolomites and of their unbelievable color actually belongs to the natural and ancient history of the land; it is a history which, however, eludes the precise and perhaps cold framing of science when explored with the vivid eye of imagination and with the curiosity aroused by what is unknown and far off in time.

With this view, the mysterious geological event of the "Monti Pallidi" is overwhelmed with the magical and suggestive atmosphere of a realm of dwarfs and sylvan creatures enclosed in the poetic corner of our hearts.

Similarly, the silvery and eternal light of the moon still filters through every object and profile, like a silent spectator to the grand events that have shaped the rocks of the Ampezzo valley and of the dolomite landscape.

The peculiar features distinguishing these rocks from the rest of the Alps were identified by the Frenchman Deodat de Dolomieu. Adventure traveller and geology-lover, he studied and performed chemical-reactive analyses on a number of samples of what he defined as "a strange calcareous stone", taken from the Isarco valley during a trip in the Italian peninsula in 1788.

It is precisely this feature, namely the presence of calcium and magnesium carbonate, that originated the unique geological event of the Dolomite and that granted it that extraordinary beauty which, overwhelming one's sight, goes beyond the limits of our hearts and dreams.

natural elements, were necessary to give a shape to this landscape of mighty boulders, of giddily steep faces, of towers and lonely pinnacles, of thinly laced profiles where the everchanging daylight, the pale moon glimmer, the vibrating pink of sunsets and the gray of rain-swollen clouds rest, generating equally ever-changing and suggestive visual effects.

In the waters of a tropical sea, the Tethys, 270 million years ago the slow formation process of the Dolomites began: gigantic heaps of detritus, coralline and organic material, deposited one on top of the other, were disrupted by ruptures, landsliding events and tectonic foldings, and then covered again with the lava coming from powerful vulcanic explosions, while the seabed inexorably fled towards the most distant depths of the earth. Different chemical events, different formation geneses, different reactions to the stress caused by natural catastrophies, different fates did the rocks of this gigantic and wavering castle undergo in time. The signs of this variety can still be found in the presence of prevailingly calcareous formation mountains (Marmolada, Altipiani di Fanes, Croda Rossa, the Antelao peak), of areas crowded with vulcanic debris (La Valle Formation, Marmolada Conglomeration), or of more recent marly material (the Ampezzo plateaus of Remeda Rossa, of Alpe di Fosses, and of Ra Stua). The Ampezzo landscape is characterized by the presence of the dolomitic rock which, 223 million years ago, originated the mighty structures of the Tre Cime di Lavaredo, the Cristallo, the Sorapis, the Pomagagnon and part of the Tofane. One last

effort was necessary to free the "Monti Pallidi" from the cosy warmth of the sea embrace.

135 million years ago, a new phase of this extraordinary event of primordial forces began: the Dolomites emerged from the water and, with them, along the complicated spiral of time, the entire chain of the Alps which, imprisoned on the bottom of the sea, was compressed, disrupted and lifted by

the uncontrollable thrust of the African continent against the Euro-Asian clod. It is the same thrust that is still acting, causing the Ampezzo peaks to rise by 6 millimeters yearly, a rise that is barely sufficient to contrast the force of erosion which, instead, removes half a centimeter of rock over the same period of time. During the long dolomitic formation period, thousands of small moving creatures, shellfish, elementary vegetable organisms, chips of coral reefs, animal imprints and skeletons remained imprisoned in the solid rock; they now remain as evidence of the slow and inexorable evolution of land and water life from then down to today.

The dolomitic rock, hostile to the process of fossilization, jealous guardian of its own secrets, has compressed, often emptied and dissolved these beings: in fact, while in the majority of cases the fossilization process entails the transformation of organic remains into stone, the Dolomite leaves us only with millenary imprints. The draw-

ings, the perfect shapes of sponges, sea-urchins, corals and shells, suddenly lead us into the magical and incredible suggestiveness of a sea landscape that disappears and grows blurred

when the dolomitic stratifications were formed, and that the people of Cortina call "Pé de Cioura", "goat hoof", because of its resemblance with the hoofprints goats leave in the mud.

in the sunny immensity of a world of rocks: the fan-shaped shell of the Daonella, a bivalve mollusk, the spindle-shaped shell of the Ammonite, a swimming mollusk of the Cefalopodi group, examined by paleonthologists for the dating of the rocks containing them; and, again, the special shell of the Megalodonte, a mollusk that existed 223 million years ago,

Man appeared long after the orogenesis of the Dolomites which, almost two million years ago, were covered by a thick layer of ice - as happened to the entire Alps and most of central-northern Europe. Life started again at the end of the last glaciation, about 15,000 years ago. The naked and plantless landscape, interrupted only by steep rocky profiles and heaps of morenic debris, began to turn green again and gurgle with fresh running water. In the thick woods of pines, firs and beeches and on the high meadowy stretches now rested deer, steinbocks, chamois ... In this environment, which promised animal preys and land fruits, the Mesolythic man arrived in the summertime (6,000 B.C.), coming up from his winter settlements along the Piave val-

ley and on the Venetian Pre-Alps.

Around Cortina d'Ampezzo on the grassy slopes of the Giau Pass, down to the Mondeval hollow, today there remain traces, yet to be studied systematically, of this presence. Under a mighty boulder which broke off the nearby Lastoni di Formin and rolled down the Mondeval hollow slopes, are the summer dwelling and burial-place of a man; he has been attributed an age of forty, around 1.67 m tall. Next to his skeleton, flintstone chips, bone and deer-horn manufacts help us recontruct the scene, rites, daily customs of men that were used to living freely amongst animals that they themselves relentlessly hunted, in the untouched and elementary world of our origins. Generations that have become a myth, thanks to the increasing going by of time and to the imagination of those who followed. Similarly, in the unuttered emotions of our feelings or in the smiling lingering on of memory, remains the image of the Ampezzo Dolomites, sculptured in their natural beauty, forever wrapped in the pale, silvery veil woven by the dwarfs to allow the Earth Prince and the Moon Princess to make their dream of love come true.

A desert landscape going back to 6000 years ago, when deer hunters ventured from the plains to higher areas that were more suitable to their activity. Like the Alpe di Mondeval, these were unpopulated areas that were used exclusively in the summer for such specific purposes. These men would spend the entire season in search of not only precious meat but also horns and skins to be traded in the valley. The big outcropping boulder under which the so-called "Mondeval man" was found is still there. Together with the perfectly preserved skeleton, many objects were found which, besides being part of the burial equipment, demonstrate that it must have been a place of habitual summer settlement for hunters.

Flintstone chips were found also in other areas, thus proving that this type of activity was widespread at that time.

The area is particularly fascinating because its elevated grasslands, against the wonderful rock-faces, seem to be suspended in time, so much have they maintained their ancient and original features and atmosphere.

Though rarely visited, it is an area that can be easily reached both from the Giau Pass and the Rifugio Palmieri, passing between Croda da Lago and Becco di Mezzodí.

8   THE MONDEVAL MAN.

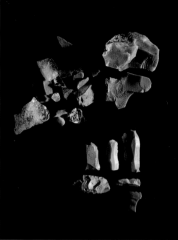

9   FLINTSTONES DATED 4000 B.C.

10   THE MONDEVAL GRASSLANDS, THE PELMO AND BECCO DI MEZZODÌ IN THE BACKGROUND.

In 450 B.C. the Paleo-Venetians arrived, probably from the Friuli area. Perhaps they were in search of metals (there is an old galena mine on the Giau Pass) when they moved up the Boite Valley.

They settled all over Cadore, at first only seasonally and later more stably. The cremation tombs found in the Cadore area at Pieve, Pozzale, Lozzo and Valle confirm their presence in the area.

As for the Ampezzo valley, systematic research in this respect has not yet been carried out. However, one can suggest that these populations ventured until Cortina and then continued towards the Pusteria valley. Evidence of this lies in a number of peculiarities of the local dialect, such as the desinences in -es in local toponomy (Crignes, Clanderies, Gotres, Socrepes), as well as in other customs such as that of marking boundaries with iron rings.

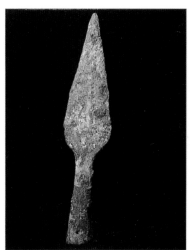

11 Tofana Terza and its stratifications.

12 Spear tip (300 b.c.).

The glacial periods buried the whole territory under a mantle reaching even 1500 m. of thickness. After every thaw, life would slowly resume and the first buds would rise from the lifeless rocks, to then become plants and trees.

Rich in refreshing water, the soil would start producing.

Meanwhile, the enormous force of the great masses of ice would befreed during the thaws and erode the hard rock, increasingly breaking it up until the deep clefts of the gorges were created.

Stone after stone, valleys were formed, while peaks and mountains took up ever-defining shapes. Today, when admiring the landscape, no thought is made of the great disruptions that created it.

But a closer look or a different interpretation of what is being observed is sufficient to get a glimpse, among the suggestive pleats of the Dolomites, of the long and tormented life they have experienced.

13   THE ZUMELLES CREST. IN THE CRISTALLO GROUP.

14   BEFORE DAWN IN THE BOITE VALLEY.

15   THE 50-METER JUMP OF RIO FANES.

In remote times, these places were covered by the pleasant warm thof a quiet sea, the Tethys, harboring many forms of life that today are imprisoned in the rock.

50 million years ago, the peaks of what are now known as the Alps emerged from this large warm sea, thrusted upwards by the mighty disruptions of the earth crust. Shells, fish, sea-urchins and corals, sponges and other sea beings have left their marks, their perfect prints in the hard dolomite rock.

Various fossils of "dicerocardium", a bivalve shell reaching up to seventy centimeters in length, were found in Val Travenanzes (photo 17). Today, such fossils, from those only a few millimeters long to the most spectacular ones, may be admired in the Museo delle Regole, thanks to the exciting and passionate work of Rinaldo Zardini. Thousands of items, catalogued in a precise and schematic manner, allow you to plunge just for a moment in that past environment, among the sea fauna of the Tethys Sea. The rock layer preserving the signs of the sea epoch emerges in various areas of the valley.

For example, in Ra Stua, just before reaching the Alpine summer hut, many ammonites can be observed in the pink rock, while in other areas the exemplaries are so tiny that it is almost impossible to spot them.

It is severely forbidden to collect fossils and this aims at safeguarding a heritage that is more interesting from a scientific viewpoint than from a tourist one.

16   THE ANCONA HOLE.

17   SPRINGTIME IN VAL TRAVENANZES DURING THAW.

In remote times, the rocks reached the valley and the landscape lacked the woods and meadows that today surround the Ampezzo valley. Very slowly, however, the organic remains dissolved in the ground and created ideal conditions for the growth of plants also in the higher areas.

The landscape changed from the coldness of a completely rocky environment to one in which the rocky peaks could be seen outcropping from green slopes. The grass first and the trees then, and on to a valley bottom completely covered with firs, larches and other plants adjusting to the climate. The Swiss pine is the tree growing on the highest elevations, as it resists cold temperatures and winds.

Thanks to its flexbility, it is the type of wood that is preferred for sculptures. Unlike those areas in which the winter climate is milder, trees at this altitude grow very slowly. In fact, though not reaching enormous dimensions, they are often over three hundred years old.

18 THE LEROSA MEADOWS WITH THE SORAPIS GROUP IN THE BACKGROUND (3205 METERS).

Rio Fanes flows on the bottom of the Fanes valley, with spectacular jumps and falls that can be reached easily on foot from Fiames. The first waterfall interrupting its flow is surrounded completely by the green of the woods and it is its whiteness, therefore, that draws ones attention.

It is an extraordinary sight, especially when crossing it by passing on a ledge just beneath the veil of water. Further down towards the valley, an "iron" trail allows the more expert to flank another fifty meter-jump in the air, and then move on to the opposite side of the rio and climb up the main trail. Lower still, Rio Fanes meets the stream coming from Val Travenanzes. The almost seventy-meter-deep gorge is crossed by a legendary wooden bridge, rightly called the "High Bridge". The legend tells that, having reached the edge of the ravine, such was the desire of a horseman to reach his beloved one, that he crossed the gorge with one single jump.

20   PASSAGE UNDER THE FANES WATERFALL.

21   AFTER A RAINFALL, A LARCH BRANCH.

22   THE FIRST WATERFALL OF RIO FANES.

Over the centuries, the nakedness of the rocks has yielded completely different results. On one hand, the tormented roots of a Swiss pine are evidence of the struggle for survival in a yet difficult environment. On the other, the delicacy and fragility of a mountain flower that has managed to make its way among the rocks. Elsewhere, such as under the Lastoni di Formin, behind Croda da Lago (photo 25), the ground still needs many centuries to be covered with green.

23 THE ROOTS OF A SWISS PINE.

24 THE "SOLDANELLA".

25 THE SCREE AND PINNACLES OF CRODA DA LAGO.

What used to be only a crossing area or seasonal settlement area is now one of the most beautiful places in the world.

THE LANDSCAPE

AMONG ROCK-FACES, WOODS AND SILENCES, TO BE DISCOVERED ON FOOT.

It is not only one single element that makes the Ampezzo valley unique in the Dolomitic arch. Indeed, many elements are involved. Arriving from Cadore, an immediate feeling of beauty is aroused by the sight of the peaks, a feeling that grows more and more intense as one ventures into the Boite Valley. Almost a crescendo, after skimming over the dark woodland domes of Longarone and after lingering over the rose-colored rocks surrounding Tai and Valle - when the Pelmo and Antelao greet the arriving traveller - one's eyes open, overwhelmed with surprise, unto an absolutely uncommon scene.

Not one, but each of the peaks surrounding the Ampezzo valley has something in which to excel: the lone impressiveness of Tofana di Rozes, the protective face of the Pomagagnon, culminating in the clear brightness of the Cristallo, the superb rocky profiles of the Faloria, the distant moon-atmosphere of Croda da Lago, emerging from the dark tangled mass of thick woodland slopes ... Such peculiarities, however, merge into one single gasp of absolute beauty. As if the matter of ice and rock of each mountain reflected each other and penetrated one into the other, transported by the sunlight and by the force of the wind.

Arriving from the north, instead, from the dark road at the bottom of the valley wedging in woods and under the rock layer, a sigh of relief is certainly aroused by the spaciousness of the landscape. After the oppression brought about by the winding curves, suddenly and finally the airiness of the valley of Cortina with its range of colors and elements; and above it, the enormous strip of sky that disappears down there, towards the lowland. And on the left, the essential elegance of Punta Fiames, which seems to have broken away from the slender diaphragm of the Pomagagnon, never daring to part completely and definitely, remaining anchored to it as if by magic.

Eastwards, after a first fleeting view of the Cortina valley, arriving from the Tre Croci Pass, one remains in a limbo situation for quite a while. Up to Alverà, the highest neighborhood of Cortina on this side of the valley, the road continues, endlessly shadowed by the woody slopes of the Faloria which, descending and climbing again in a vast horizon of larches, continuously come between the traveller and his destination; and they seem to want to keep alive the ancient legend whereby the Faloria Mountain guarded the

Doorway to the house of God Silvano, the place from which the sun god rose every morning.
But the wait is rewarded because, as soon as the woods thin out to give way to the Mietres meadows, suddenly, also the first houses appear, some of which are amongst the oldest of the village, together with the little church of S. Giuliana, a miniature anticipation of the center of Cortina.

Falzarego probably offers the most all-embracing view of Ampezzo, a synthesis perhaps of the impressions that one gets when arriving from the other three cardinal points.

The Lagazuoi prelude, with its peak reached by a modern and spectacular cableway balanced on a cable without intermediate towers, is the "trait d'union" between the splendid Dolomites of Val Badia and the Cordevole Valley on one side and Cortina on the other.

The fascination aroused by the steep slope of Tofana di Rozes, which painfully protected the Italian troops during the First World War, is appeased by the landscape - almost a plateau, the Cianzope' - spreading up to the right. Similar to the remains of a legendary castle, the Cinque Torri, a training area for rock-climbers of all levels, rise from the thick woods that have grown on the crushed heaps of an old landslide.

However, continuing down the road, the traveller's surprise

turns into unutterable enchantment when, past the tunnel dug under the Pocol, the entire Ampezzo valley opens wide all around. Sight is priviledged from this observation point and this seems to be suggested by the certainly not recent presence of a square which allows tourists to stop and admire the landscape and snap photographs of it.

The amazing equilibrium of the peaks and the feeling of protection that they arouse, though never becoming oppressive, the almost calculated distribution of sky, rock, woods and meadows and, lastly, the clustering of the houses around the white bell-tower, come together in the form of countless images crowding up one's eyes and mind with feelings and thoughts that can hardly be separated one from the other but that, at the same time, are overbearing and undeniable in their uniqueness.

And it is not anymore only the beautiful mountains, the beautiful colors, or the beautiful houses that grant Cortina its regal charm, but their merging together in an extraordinary and ever-changing harmony.
The creation of such a combina-

tion, besides the dominant intervention of nature, was performed also by man who, though opening the doors of his casket to the world, has been actively concerned about guarding his precious treasure jealously. And if, at the peak of the high season, the line of cars recalls the city environment, it is nevertheless true that the woods have not been "torn apart" everywhere to create ski slopes, nor have the old roads in the woods been opened to modern jeep traffic, nor have the ski lifts been enhanced to "churn out" thousands of winter sportsmen every hour. On the contrary, on March 22, 1990 the Dolomiti d'Ampezzo Natural Park was constituted. Covering quite a large part of the territory, the natural safeguard area falls under the jurisdiction of the "Regole d'Ampezzo" (Ampezzo Rules) - the centuries-old institution of Cortina -, a condition ensuring the same spirit of ancient wisdom which has protected the valley over the centuries. Thus, the Veneto Region has decided to officially acknowledge the respect that nature in this area deserves, although the innate spirit of the Ampezzo people, who have always protected and guarded their local natural heritage, would not have made this step necessary. To the Ampezzo dweller, the woods, meadows and land have always been his primary means of sustenance and this bond has remained intact as of today. Even in the breathless "house race", the Local Government has constantly imposed restrictions of all kinds.
Typologies must be in line with the old Ampezzo architectural styles, buildings cannot exceed specific dimensions and, although the breadth of the valley could have allowed for greater urban expansion, meadows have been preserved from constructions and the number of houses has remained unvaried for many years now. The fresh green of the meadows is echoed by the strong color of the woods; the white walls of the houses respond to the thousands of hues of the wooden balconies; the darker Giau rocks seem to try toning down the dazzling light of the Cristallo; the brightness of the blue sky is drawn by the clear outline of those gray-pink pinnacles that arrogantly fill our sight. As has already been said, this careful proportion of elements becomes in itself the symbol and synthesis of the beauty and uniqueness of the Queen of the Dolomites.

In other mountain resorts, woods and meadows cover the majority of the slopes, while only the higher parts of the peaks shed the green of the trees to reveal the naked rock. In Cortina, the rocks slope down to the valley meadows, increasing the equilibrium of proportions of the Ampezzo landscape and, at the same time, eliminating that vague feeling of remote distance that the other dolomitic horizons instil. On the contrary, one has the feeling he can stretch out his arm and let the gravel that time has eroded from the faces of Tofana di Mezzo, or the snow that has remained imprisoned among the artistic layers of the Cristallo, slip through his fingers. All one has to do to make these feelings come true is stroll down the old railway trail, thus passing from houses to meadows, woods and gravels, down to the Rio Felizon gorge.

Or one simply plunges into the thin larch woods down the Faloria slopes or, again, follows the trail that continues along the same level under Cadini della Tofana to reach the Posporcora Pass and Col Rosà.

When the sun joins in, then the games of contrast are multiplied because the views are multiplied and, together with the general three-dimensionality, thousands of other small dimensions join in, revealing every single pleat of this magically petrified fabric. Thus, one

has the feeling that his eyes can caress the curves of the rock, penetrating it at every different height, to later emerge again in yet another protrusion, in a new spike, and resume passing through its most secret clefts with enchanted eyes.

Those who love Cortina and have spent some time there, also during the low season, despite most shops and restaurants being shut, are aware of the indescribable variety of effects that the sun creates during the day, over the various yearly periods, with the snow reflection or the heat of the summer air; and they are magically guided by this love experience, constantly turned towards the peak which, in that particular situation, in that particular season, at that precise hour of the day, offers the most extraordinary sight.

Every hour has its mountain, because the position of the sun, the angulations of the rocks, the different textures and shapes create the same countless pictorial and plastic effects, highlighting in particular now one now another peak. There are moments during the day when even the whitest peak of Cortina, the bell-tower of the parish church, lights up, reflecting the bright sunlight on its candid stone. It is not of dolomite, it was not born of nature, but its position is unquestioned, its role being rooted almost as much as that of the mountains surrounding it. Imagining Cortina without its bell-tower is like imagining it without the Tofane, without Croda da Lago, like a Cortina without the Cristallo.

The sweetness of some of the mountain life expressions seems to be in contrast with the wild background environment. The Popena, Cristallo and Creste Bianche Group (photo 32) looks like an unsurpassable barrier, when seen from the north. Actually, it can be crossed along various paths and "iron" trails and, even during the wintertime, marvellous alpinistic skiing outings allow the entire northern flank to be enjoyed.

The peak of the Cristallo was reached for the first time by Paul Grohmann in 1865, together with Santo Siorpaes and Angelo Dimai. The massif still preserves two glaciers, evidence of the glacial epochs: the first one, at 2,800 meters, under the peak of the Cristallo, where Michele Innerkofler fell, and the second one, the one of the Cresta Bianca, from 2,600 to 2,800 meters in height.

These peaks witnessed bloodshedding battles between

Austria and Italy during the First World War. In fact, all over these areas, remains of camps, trenches and barbed wire entanglements are often encountered.

32 The CRISTALLO GROUP AND THE CRESTE BIANCHE VIEWED FROM PRATO PIAZZA.

Seen from Cortina (photo 36), the Cristallo group is worth its name: under the sunrays, every single one of its layers glitters like a precious stone and the rounded profiles loom up against the blue sky as if they were the contours of a jewel without equal.

Seen from its northern flank, instead, (photo 33), it offers a completely different sight: the rock creates mighty towers, deep channels and precipituous screes. Seen from Lake Landro (photo 35), it gives the impression of closing the valley, allowing for no opening whatsoever towards the south. Actually, it can be circled by crossing the Tre Croci Pass or the Cimabanche Pass.

33   THE POPENA PEAK (M. 3152).

34   THE THAW.

35   LAKE LANDRO.

36   THE BARN FARTHEST UP IN ALVERÀ TOWARDS THE CRISTALLO.

Cortina's most famous massif is that of the Tofane: Tofana di Rozes, di Mezzo and Terza. They all exceed 3,200 meters in height. Tofana di Rozes is more isolated and rises mightily (photo 41), with its southern face measuring a difference in height of over 800 meters; it is renowned amongst alpinists for its numerous "routes", among which the first climb opened by the Etvos baronesses is quite remarkable, not to speak of other superb, though extremely difficult, routes. The wounds left by the two fronts of the First World War are still evident also on the Tofane: first among all is the Castelletto mine. At the foot of Punta Giovannina (photo 38), between Tofana di Rozes and Tofana di Mezzo, saddled on the stones, is Rifugio Giussani.

Few persons know about the valley that runs behind the Tofane: Val Travenanzes, of rare and wild beauty, full of crystal clear sources, of meadows, screes and gorges. It starts from Forcella Col Dei Bos and ends in Pian de Loa (Piana del Lupo = Wolf's Plain). Between Tofana di Mezzo and Tofana Terza is one of the still existing glaciers of the massif: it has now become quite small and can be reached from the peak of Tofana di Mezzo, along an "iron" trail.

38   THE LAST SUN ON TOFANA DI MEZZO.

39   EVIDENCE OF THE FIRST WORLD WAR.

37   TOFANA TERZA.

41   THE MIGHTY SOUTHERN FACE OF TOFANA DI ROZES AT DAWN (RIGHT).

Originally, Croda da Lago probably was a single, compact massif. Geological events, as well as wind and rain erosion, have broken it up, changing it into a wall of sharp pointed pinnacles, almost like the wall of a medieval fortress.

Campanile Federa, Campanile Innerkofler, Croda da Lago, Cima d'Ambrizzola, Ago da Lago, Punta Fraio and Torre d'Abete: these are the names of some of the peaks, so pointed that they allow merely the possibility of standing on them for one short exciting moment.

The tormented shape of the rock further stresses the mountain's ever-changing features when hit by light: from the pale gray at noon, highlighted by the dark green of the underlying woods, to the flaming red of the evening, when the pinnacles actually turn into

42   THE SHARP PINNACLES OF CRODA DA LAGO AT SUNSET.

climbing flames rising from the
black of the shadowed trees.

The long and winding road that links Misurina to Rifugio Auronzo plays a fundamental role in the popularity of the Tre Cime di Lavaredo. After all, who has never heard of them or seen them on the most refined publications, on dolomitic hotel brochures, on the postcards of the beginning of the century or on the most recent ones? The charm of these three giants thrusted into the screes, motionless in their loneliness, is absolutely unresistable.

There are three mountain huts built around the Tre Cime: the "Auronzo", which can be reached also by car, the small "Tre Cime", which seems even smaller because it is under the dizzying "Spigolo Giallo", but especially the "Locatelli", from which one can catch a magical, fabulous glimpse of these three giants.

43 The Tre Cime di Lavaredo viewed from the Paterno screes.

From the Lavaredo saddle (photo 44), the impressive northern faces appear in their wholeness and majestic mightiness. The entire yellow-pink part has maintained the original color of the Dolomite, as it has never ben touched by rain: this indicates that the face inclination is even more than perpendicular.

These were faces that, until a few decades ago, were considered absolutely unaccessible.

Two young Ampezzo men, the Dimai brothers, together with Emilio Comici, exploded this myth in the 1930s, when they opened the first route on the yellow slabs of the northern face of Cima Grande.

Already in 1911, the great Preuss reached Cima Piccolissima in free climb, thus introducing a new climbing philosophy. The exact opposite of Preuss, four Germans, in the middle of the winter and with the help of hundreds of expansion nails that they hammered into the rock for fourteen days, opened the famous and controversial perfectly vertical Via a Goccia d'Acqua, also called Via dei Colibrí.

In between these two extremes, mention has to be made of the "Cassin", the "Via degli Scoiattoli" to Grandi Tetti and the "Couzy" routes to Cima Ovest. Even non-expert alpinists have the possibility of reaching the peaks of the Grande and of the Ovest di Lavaredo, along two routes of average difficulty.

44   THE NORTHERN FACES VIEWED FROM THE LAVAREDO SADDLE.

46   THE CRODA PASSAPORTO RIDGE.

45   YELLOW POPPIES, OFTEN ENCOUNTERED IN SCREES.

47   THE TRE CIME VIEWED FROM THE "CAPANNA DEI PASTORI" HUT.

The sight of the sunset seen from the peak of the Lagazuoi is undoubtedly without equal. At this time of the day, the valleys disappear in the shadows, thus highlighting the pinnacles which, still exposed to the red sunlight, take up colors that are at the least extraordinary. The more the sun sets on the horizon, the more intense darkness becomes on the bottom of the valley; therefore, the peaks seem to be lit almost by an internal source of light, taking possession of the sunset light and becoming white-hot.
Then, the sun disappears and the spell is broken: everything goes back to normal and the contrast fades away in the darkness.

49   SUNSET ON THE LAGAZUOI.

51   THE AVERAU AND THE PELMO.

50   THE RIFUGIO LAGAZUOI (2,756 METERS) AND THE CIVETTA (ON THE RIGHT).

53 THE LAKE AT CRODA DA LAGO (2,046 METERS).

54 NIGHT BIRD OF PREY.

55 LARCH WOOD.

Closing the Ampezzo valley on the southern flank, the Antelao is typical for its slanted slabs which, turned northwards, always bear traces of snow. It is only by passing under it that one realizes how mighty this mastodon is, when it seems to plunge in the woods which take up the same hues of the rocks in autumn.

With its feathered helmet, it has deserved its title of King of the Dolomites, undisputed ruler over the entire Boite valley, viewable from Cortina to beyond Pieve di Cadore. Its eastern glacier is also marvellous as, jutting out towards Val d'Oten, it looks at the Marmarole Group.

56 THE ANTELAO AT SUNSET (3,263 METERS).

The Sorapis is a peak that has in some way been neglected by the majority of visitors, who often forget about it when compared to nearby Monte Faloria and the big Antelao. The only site receiving many summer visitors is the Rifugio Vandelli which has gained its fame thanks to its splendid mountain lake. Similar to an emerald cut in the rock, it reflects the elegant profile of "God's Finger" in its splendid and eternally ice-cold waters. Conoisseurs of the "historic" peaks of Cortina, however, love the great frozen throne of the Sorapis (photo 57) that seems suspended on the borderline

with the blue sky.
It is one of the few glaciers exposed to sunrays that still resists increasingly mild temperatures.

57   THE PEAK OF THE SORAPIS WITH ITS SNOW-FIELD (3,205 M).

Lake Da Lago (photo 61), frequent destination of excursionists, owes its great fame to the splendid scenario surrounding it. From here, not even Cortina can be sighted, as it remains hidden by the trees. Only the lunar background of Becco di Mezzodí and the profile of the Sleeping Beauty. To its side, the steep face of Croda da Lago. The enchantment of the lake is even greater when considering that, in no matter what climatic condition - drought, winter, summer - its level remains mysteriously unchanged, maybe thanks to an underground spring of which, as of today, still no trace has been found. Next to the lake, Rifugio Palmieri contributes to the area's suggestiveness: one of the oldest mountain huts in the Valley, it maintains intact all the charm of the style that was typical of the end of last century.

59 A STREAM.

60 RIO TRAVENANZES.

61 THE LAKE OF CRODA DA LAGO WITH BECCO DI MEZZODÌ.

The highest mountain in the Dolomites is the Marmolada (3342 m.) with its mighty glacier, destination of skiers at all times of the year. It can be seen from the Falzarego Pass, in between the black volcanic rocks - the oldest in the area - of Mount Padon.

A fifty-minute car drive from Cortina leads to one of its peaks, Punta Rocca, from which the sight is actually one of three hundred and sixty degrees. Peaks and valleys follow one another endlessly in all directions, almost as if to crown the Queen of the Dolomites.

62   THE GREAT MARMOLADA MASSIF (3342 M.) VIEWED FROM THE FALZAREGO PASS.

The area towards San Vigilio di Marebbe and Braies has quite a unique feature: high meadows, with no vertical faces bounding them. Only grass, pines, dwarf pines and outcropping stratifications of small rocks. Lago di Fosses (photo 65) stands out even more in autumn when the light blue color of its waters breaks away from the burnt red of the grass.

Croda del Becco, with its white slabs, naturally marks the limits of the two valleys and allows one's sight to embrace both the Ampezzo Valley and Lago di Braies with the Pusteria Valley.

This is the kingdom of steinbocks, while, further down, where the woods can protect them, live the roe deer. Their ability to mimic in the environment when autumn comes is amazing.

63 A ROEBUCK.

64 AUTUMN MIMETISM.

65 LAKE FOSSES. CRODA DEL BECCO IN THE BACKGROUND (2,810 M).

66 CRODA ROSSA (3146 M) VIEWED FROM THE LEROSA MEADOWS.

Croda Rossa looks like a wounded and bleeding giant. Its color is so peculiar that it has made of it the leading actor of many legends among which ....

67 A SMALL STRAWBERRY.

68 A CENTURIES-OLD SWISS PINE.

41

Lake Misurina is quite large for its altitude. Nevertheless, its sheet of water is barely sufficient to reflect the magnificence of the Sorapis (photo on the side) dominating the landscape, despite the distance. On one side, the woods die out in the water; on the other, the Dolomites Road leads to the grand hotels of the beginning of the century. On the occasion of the 1956 Olympic Games, the frozen lake was used for speed skating races on a track of over 400 meters, that had been sawed off at the edge of the frozen surface and, thus, for safety reasons, transformed into a single enormous floating island

69 LAKE MISURINA (1775 M).

THE HISTORY

FASCINATING AND UNIQUE FOR OVER 1000 YEARS...

The stone profiles, pinnacles and laced circle of the window-sill delicately weave mullioned windows that make the soaring bell-tower seem even lighter towards the top, where it culminates in a golden sphere reflecting the colors of the sky: it is the bell-tower that has always been the visual reference point for those entering the Ampezzo valley, for those receiving greeting cards from Cortina, for those who nostalgically look at early suggestive photographs of the valley. Today, as it was in the past. Even before the new bell-tower was built (1852-1858), the one that can be seen today, at a time in which structures were still being built in wood, and even before that, going back in the centuries, before the church was completely rebuilt in 1773, the bells have always struck the hours of the day, of daily moments and rests, of the season changes, of the going by of the years. This central feature of the church was reflected in the real and profound religiousness of the Ampezzo dwellers who still give evidence of it in the lasting abundance of traditions, in their custom to prayer and to the ritual celebration of all feasts, in the bonds between the people's everyday life and everyday moves and the sounds of the church: the bell tolls accompanied the farmers to the fields, they ploughed the turbulent stormy skies, or warned of imminent heavy snowfalls, while the men gathered the horses to haul the snow-plough.

The first documented memory

of a church existing in Ampezzo, the church of San Giacomo, dates back to the year 1208, at the time of the dispute between the mother church of Cadore, the church of Pieve and the peripheral churches in the area, which wanted authorization to administer the Sacraments autonomously. The church of San Giacomo became the parish church of Ampezzo probably around the year 1347 and what it looked like then is unknown. Certainly, however, the religious feelings of the Ampezzo community, since those remote times, were expressed only in the desire to make their place of prayer and hope a significant and solemn place, a place where the unitary spirit of the community materialized in a higher and more sublime sphere.

In 1355, the church of S. Caterina was erected on the northern front of the square facing the present parish church. According to A. Illing, the cult of S. Caterina della Ruota could be evidence of the evolution of an ancient pagan cult, obscure and remote like the people who brought it to the Ampezzo valley and that have been buried by time itself, by the wavering balance of the stones and by the legacies that have settled one over the other and that were left by those who followed. Yet it seems that the bright energy of the sun, adored by the Celts who spread over the Po Valley around the year 400 B.C. and ventured as far as the Boite Valley, flowed into the wheel accompanying the portrayal of S. Caterina. The contacts with the Celts, after all, deeply changed the Ampezzo culture, influencing its tongue, customs and daily rites: for example, the custom of tracing boundaries with iron rings, or the "perarguò" rite, widespread until last century, which propitiated the abundance of future crops by tossing burning sheaves of hay in the fields on the night of the fifth of January, or the exploitation of

common pastures on community territories. All traces of other ancient settlements in the Ampezzo valley, even those dating back to the Roman Ages, were anyway buried by the disruptive mass of rocks which broke away from Mount Cristallo between the V and VI century A.D., a landslide which, sweeping away rubbles, soil and trees, settled at the bottom of the valley, where the Boite meets the Bigontina.

The arrival of the Longobards, who from the Friuli area went as far as Cadore and then the Boite Valley, was determining, although scarsely testified. According to the reconstructions of historians, it was probably during this period that the Regole organization, namely the common administration of the Ampezzo valley pastures first and woods later, was established.

This tradition is certainly of barbarian origin, since there is no trace whatsoever of it in the Roman or Germanic laws.

The erection of the Boitestein stronghold, later known as the Podestagno, was dated back to the same period of the Longobard settlement; it was the bulwark defending the entire history of Cortina and Cadore, to which this history was indissolubly linked until the year 1521, when the handing over of Cortina to the Hapsburg Emperor was ratified, while Cadore remained Venetian. Despite this transfer from the Serenissima to Austria, which was not the only one in the history of Cortina, there is a peculiar feature of the valley organization making it almost "super partes": not considering the central government it depended on, Ampezzo always managed to maintain an extremely elevated degree of autonomy, to the point that, for example, it never had the duty of sending its young men to war to defend one or the other central government, and that the Regole were always allowed to act undisturbed, on the basis of their Laudi, or regulations, in the territorial management of the valley.

Therefore, over the ninety years spent under the Doge's Vicar, over the three centuries spent under the Bottestagno Captain, appointed by the Austrian Emperor, over the other two cen-

turies spent under today's Italy, Cortina never lost its independent spirit and never became Austrian or Venetian, but simply remained Cortina. For over two and a half centuries, after Venice had lost Bottestagno and Ampezzo, the history of Cortina lacked events, if not small rivalries or new friendships with the "neighboring valleys". Not that these were unimportant, on the contrary: they were

of fundamental importance in defining the Ampezzo valley boundaries, especially those with S. Vito, below the Giau Pass, which kept diplomats and less-diplomats so busy until the year 1827.

During the three centuries of Archducal Ampezzo or Imperial Ampezzo, Cortina strengthened its administrative organization, it became wealthy, the number of its inhabitants grew, passing from 1200-1300 persons to over 2000 in the eighteenth century, the defence of its woods, the valley treasure, became systematic. Peace ended when Napoleon arrived in Austria and Italy: in 1797, the war between France and the Serenissima reached the gates of Ampezzo. The French advanced until Pieve; the Austrians, on the other side, barricaded themselves around Bottestagno but, almost magically, Cortina remained unharmed. At least by skirmishes and battles. Because, actually, the fleeing Austrian soldiers asked for refuge in their nearest bulwark, and robberies in the churches were not so rare, after all.

However, it was in the year 1805 that Cortina was involved also politically: the Pressburg Peace Treaty established that the Tyrol, and Ampezzo with it, were to be donated to Bavaria, a mere cat's paw to Napoleon. The Bavarians interfered more with Ampezzo and, after them, only three years later, the Isarco Circle, with Bressanone as its capital, did the same.

In 1809, Napoleon's Great War broke out, with Ampezzo finding itself right between the Franco-Bavarians and the Austrians. The consequences were devastating: the valley continued to be the crossing place for troops now of one faction and then of the other, until the tragic fire in the village -- which was yet another opportunity to demonstrate solidarity amongst the Ampezzo valley dwellers --; for three years it belonged to Napoleon's Empire, and then returned to Austria in 1813. Years of sadness and hunger followed,

until it became a crossing point with the construction of the Alemagna Road, cheerfully inaugurated by Francis I of Austria, and a resort area honored by the visits of the Emperor himself.

The reconstruction of the bell-tower dates back to this period and was not caused by aestethic reasons - although it would have deserved them - but by practical ones: some stones had broken off the main structure, thus running the risk of killing passer-bys, and unusual creaking sounds disturbed the bell-cell. In 1850 the construction of the new bell-tower began, on the basis of a project drawn up by a Viennese engineer, Erminio Bergmann. Starting from this period, Cortina expanded touristically and, as the new century began, it became the destination of alpine expeditions, bob-sleigh races, headquarters of the Ski Club since 1903, and opened up to the rest of the Dolomites thanks to the new Falzarego Road.
Unfortunately, the golden and pioneering period of the Cortina

of the beginning of the twentieth century was disrupted by the new war, the Great War, which turned the surrounding mountains into tragic battlefields. In 1914, the young Ampezzo men were called to arms and, in 1915, Cortina was occupied by the Italian troops. Descriptions of the blood-shedding battles fought at high elevations are reported in the book "La Guerra delle Tofane", a tragic evidence of the sufferance that annexation to Italy cost Cortina. But peace came, and with peace, its fame of renowned alpine resort returned. In 1921 the Calalzo-Cortina-Dobbiaco railway was activated, thus linking the Po Valley directly to the Pusteria Valley and, therefore, to Austria. The first Two-man Bobsleigh World Championships were held, the "Scoiattoli", the society of Cor-

tina alpinists, were borne, the Hockey Club was founded. One more war was left to be waged until present days, and once again Cortina was the battlefield: in 1943 it was occupied by the Germans, although in 1945 it was liberated by the Americans, and by 1947 it was reconfirmed within the province of Belluno.
The 1956 Olympic Games are the higlight of this synthesis of

the history of Ampezzo, opening a completely new chapter in which Cortina d'Ampezzo becomes synonym of sports, fashion, amusements and lush and radiant nature.

The tiny village of Staolin (photo 76) reminds of one of those old paintings in which Cortina was only a tiny cluster of houses.
It rises on an old landslide that can still be recognized from the wavy contour of the ground. In past times, the village did not exist and only small clusters of few houses, today's neighborhoods, could be spotted in the valley, each with its tiny church. The surrounding land, toilfully disforested for agricultural purposes, was the most precious treasure for survival.
 This notion of the importance of land is still preserved in the guiding spirit of the Ampezzo Regole, which date back to the year 1200. According to this organization, Ampezzo's territorial heritage was mostly communitary and undivisible, and exploitable by single individuals according to the needs of each person.

76　THE LITTLE VILLAGE OF STAOLIN UNDER THE VERTICAL FACES OF THE POMAGAGNON.

In a defensive position on the saddle spur between the Boite and Rio Felizon, the Castle of Podestagno, from the German "Boitestein", meaning "stone on the Boite", played an extremely important role in the long history of Ampezzo. Maybe it was of Longobard origin; what is for sure is that the castle captain was the highest external autority. The sword of one of such captains (photo 77) can be viewed in the Museo delle Regole.

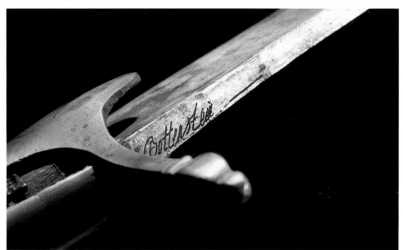

77   THE ANCIENT SWORD OF THE PODESTAGNO CASTLE.

78   THE FACADE OF THE OLD TOWN HALL OF CORTINA.

The first news relating about boundary disputes date back to the year 1300. Over the centuries, this matter became increasingly important because of the presence, shouldering the local municipalities of Ampezzo and San Vito, of what were, at that time, superpowers: the Serenissima and, from the beginning of 1500, the Austrian Empire.

Towards the end of 1700, the boundary was definitely set to eventually ease down, finally, all disputes and accidents between the two municipalities. The boundary stone bore the two respective stone symbols: Saint Marc's Lion and the symbol of the Austrian Empire (photo 79). These unique marble "marks", in the rock, can still be seen today: following their traces and discovering them is certainly an unusual and exciting experience.

Acknowledging and actually feeling the presence of man and of his centuries-old history even in places that are so difficult to reach, beaten up by the wind and exposed to the merciless erosion of time, is a unique experience.

79 THE OLD BOUNDARY (1753) BETWEEN THE "SERENISSIMA" AND THE TYROL AT THE FOOT OF THE GUSELLA.

The first document mentioning the existence of a church in Ampezzo dates back to the year 1203. But the most important one in terms of religiousness of the people was perhaps the church of S. Caterina, erected in 1353, on the site where Hotel de la Poste today stands. The marvellous door-altar sculptured by Michael Parth in the fifteenth century is preserved today in the little church of Campo di Sopra.

80   THE LITTLE CHURCH OF ALVERÀ (OIL PAINTING DATED 1845).

81   THE OLD ROAD LEADING TO CORTINA.

82   THE MARVELLOUS DOOR-ALTAR DEDICATED TO S. CATERINA AND SCULPTURED IN 1540 BY M. PARTH.

51

The Ampezzo valley, as it is today, is certainly very different from what it probably looked like to the wayfarers of the past, when the woodland limits were much closer to the rocks, thus leaving a much more extended surface covered with meadows, which allowed for greater agricultural exploitation of the valley.

The impression must have been one of catching a deep breath, especially when arriving from the narrower Cadore valley.

This is how the Dominican monk Felix Faber Schmidt saw Cortina as he returned from the Holy Land in 1484. The words he used to describe the Cortina of that time, at sunset, remain memorable: "Sole autem occasum petente venimus in pratinum, et est locus laetissimus inter montana, in quo sunt prata multa et bestiarum pascua et in medio grandis villa ..."

The Giau pasture area (photo 85) was the reason underlying the relentless discussions between the Ampezzo Rule of Ambrizzola and the San Vito one of Mondeval, called also Festornigo. This controversy continued over the centuries, more or less harshly, though never shedding blood. The land below the Giau Pass topographically belonged to the Ampezzo valley but, juridically, it was San Vito's property. In 1331, the first San Vito livestock trespassings occurred to the damage of the Ampezzo township. To suppress the struggle between sheperds, the two townships decided to solve the conflict immediately by setting the boundaries "starting from a high cleft called Gusella, behind the big rock of the Autruio summer hut and, continuing from the Gusella along a straight line, behind the same summer hut, until the great crevice where the crosses are marked ..."

However, trespassings on both sides continued regularly as did the disputes. In 1580, the rivalry seemed to be aggravated also because of matters relating to the exploitation of woods for timber. Despite the many attempts made to reach an agreement and which ended with Ampezzo acknowledging the ownership of San Vito over the Giau, in 1600 the old and ill-appeased grudges were awoken by the problem of the right to pass through the area; moreover, in 1700, the discovery of an iron-rich galena mine on the slopes of Col Piombino added further reason for dispute. In 1753 an agreement was reached between the Viennese and Venetian authorities. The people of San Vito, already settled on the Giau, were ordered to build a "... slag measuring six feet in height ...", a wall that would prevent herd trespassing. This wall can still to be seen today along the hairpin curves of the road that now leads to the Giau Pass.

84 WOODS ON THE WAY TOWARDS MANDRES.

85 BOUNDARY STONE BETWEEN THE TERRITORIES OF CORTINA AND SAN VITO.

Cortina has always enjoyed privileges relating to the management of its territory and, in general, has always been exempted from a number of fiscal and drafting duties. Municipal records show a great deal of evidence of this, among which the parchment (photo 86) of Rudolf II (1552-1612), the Austrian Emperor who confirmed the privileges which Cortina enjoyed and which it was so fond of. Such autonomy materialized over the centuries and the territory of Cortina was managed directly by the Regole of Ampezzo, with no interference or intrusion on the part of central authorities.

87   THE FURTHEST MEADOWS IN CHIAMULERA.

86   ANCIENT PARCHMENT BEARING RUDOLF II'S SEAL (1598).

88   THE SUMMER HUT AT RA STUA.

Mr. Giovanni Maria de Zanna, a thoroughbred Ampezzo dweller, bravely fought against the Turks and in support of the Emperor of Austria. His deeds were so corageous that Leopold I decided to reward him and, on January 3rd, 1692, the Emperor personally granted him the title of nobility "of the Holy Trinity and of Pietra Reale". When he returned to Cortina, he decided that such a title deserved an equally prestigious house. So, in 1699, he began the construction of the De Zanna Castle (photo 91). But things were far from being easy for him: the people of Ampezzo, for long accustomed to an equal sharing of opportunities, could not conceive such a privileged position. It seems that, at night, what had been built during the day was demolished, until the nobleman himself had to renounce his purpose.

Today, what is left of the castle in Majon are two towers, part of the surrounding walls but, most important of all, the little church of SS. Trinità, where prestigious works such as the three wooden altars and an altar-piece attributed to Palma il Giovane (1544-1628) are preserved.

89 THE CLOCK OF THE PARISH CHURCH DATED 1777.

90 LACEDEL IN A PAINTING OF THE END OF THE EIGHTEENTH CENTURY.

91 ONE OF THE TOWERS OF THE DE ZANNA CASTLE (1699).

Unlike what is happening today, namely that comfort and comodity are the leading criteria of all enterprises, roads in the past were not aimed at fast vehicles but, rather, followed the most logical and short route which was often also the steepest one. At the beginning of the 20th century, the construction of the Dolomites Road began, to easily link the various valleys among themselves. Along the old road that from Dobbiaco leads to Cortina, there was even an inn for shelter and free overnight stays for those going to the Holy Land to fight alongside the Crusaders. Since then, this route was interrupted by a rest area that is still called "Ospitale".

93   A FARMHOUSE IN MELERES.   94   THE ROAD ARRIVING TO CORTINA FROM POCOL.

It was the year 1744 when Bartolomeo Gilardoni was born in Cortina. It is said that he was a clock-maker like his father had been, but fate and his ingeniousness took him far away to the great Vienna. The archives of the Arms Preserver of the Museum of History in Vienna indicate that the man from Cortina presented Emperor Joseph II with the design of a breech-loading rifle and of a compressed air one, capable of "shooting 20 lead pellets in a few seconds at a distance of 120 steps". It was an extraordinary invention if one considers the amount of time that was then necessary to reload a traditional rifle. It even seems that, once the news of the discovery became widespread, the other armies tried to declare it illegal, since it would not have allowed the enemy "to fight on equal terms". He constructed over 1300 which can today be admired in various museums all over Europe. Bartolomeo Gilardoni from Cortina died just outside Vienna in 1799, without ever becoming rich or famous.

96   THE KEYBOARD OF AN ORGAN DATED 1777.

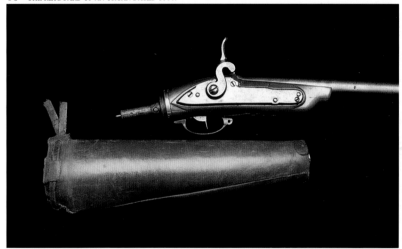

97   COMPRESSED AIR TANK FOR RIFLE.

95   A TIPICAL HOUSE IN LACEDEL.

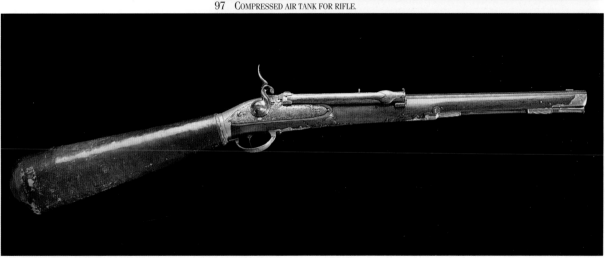

98   COMPRESSED AIR RIFLE INVENTED IN 1779 BY BARTOLOMEO GILARDONI.

CORTINA
THE VISITORS
FROM THE EARLY ENGLISHMEN OF THE PAST CENTURY TO CURRENT TOURISM.

Past thick-shadowed woods, the dusty road unexpectedly curved towards a bright horizon of meadows, fir trees, lofty rocky profiles woven against the blue sky. An unutterable feeling of astonishment and, suddenly, spontaneous, the desire to breathe - in your heart, your muscles, and in every fiber of your being - the purity, the elementary beauty of a newly discovered world! Perhaps, this is how Paul Grohmann felt when he first arrived in the Ampezzo valley in 1862. When the coach arrived in the village center, a cluster of houses gathered around the soaring peak of a white bell-tower, the young Austrian traveller got off and, looking around with enchanted eyes, lodged at the Aquila Nera of Gaetano Ghedina. Aquila Nera, Stella d'Oro, Croce Bianca, Alla Posta: names linked to travelling and meeting customs that have now disappeared, to architectural images and elements that do not exist anymore or that have been changed - in use, image, meaning - by the inexorable passing by of time. However, these are names that have been maintained in time, although they are linked to completely different ambiances and almost pioneeristic events.

They are not anymore the 3,500 overnight stays registered in 1877, but the much greater 1,250,000 of the past few years. But they remain in one's imagination and memory, capable of evoking, echoed by old photographic recollections, that already mythical atmosphere of adventure, of new and stirring discovery that probably accompanied the early foreign visitors at the end of last century. Spotted from far off by Goethe while crossing the Tridentine valleys at the end of 1700, isolatedly faced by some lone researcher such as Baron von Wulfen, a botanics-lover who reached Croda Rossa towards the end of 1790, the Dolomites and, in particular, the Ampezzo valley continued to be, until the first half of 1800, the wild and unaccessible kingdom of fairies and elfs, of creatures belonging to the woods and rocks and holding the most secret powers of nature. Be-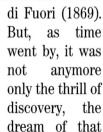cause they were brave and, especially, in need, only mountain chamois hunters with un-known names but unequalled experience could enter it. And when the Western Alps had already been conquered thanks to the romantic boldness of aristocratic English explorers, Irish John Ball climbed up the Pelmo faces in 1857, assisted and guided by a local hunter. Some years later young Paul Grohmann arrived, binding his heart and name forever to Cortina d'Ampezzo, conquering -

together with local mountaineers such as Francesco Lacedelli, Angelo Dimai and Santo Siorpaes - the yet unviolated peaks of Tofana di Mezzo (1863), Tofana di Rozes and the Sorapis (1864), the Cristallo and Tofana di Fuori (1869). But, as time went by, it was not anymore only the thrill of discovery, the dream of that first footstep to leave on the culminating peak, nor was it anymore scientific interest or naturalistic curiosity that spurred on the English, Austrian and local explorers who followed Grohmann in their climbs up the faces of those mountains.
Perhaps it was the supreme desire to test themselves, their fear and their courage, as well as the relentless power of fate. In the end, following the

thoughts and extraordinary words written by Buzzati, it must have been the longing for supreme stillness, perceived in the indestructable vertical motionlessness of the rocky structures, that urged the early alpinists on in their arduous but wonderful Cortina climbs — such a perfect and absolute quietness that the thought of death is evoked as the end of every battle and sufferance of man, the conclusion to every effort in life.

The dolomitic challenge therefore attracted English and European alpinists and thrilled the local men, the pioneers of the future generations of guides.

At the same time, it stimulated the birth and development of aristocratic and high-class tourism which, from then onwards, was to characterize the name

and charm itself of Cortina. While the guide from Sesto, Michele Innerkofler, was busy conquering the Cima Piccola di Lavaredo (1881) and alpinism, already an agonistic experience,

was evolving to take up the form of customary winter climbs and early risky free-climbing, Cortina was growing rich in hotels: the Miramonti (1904), the Cristallo (1905), the Bellevue, and the first mountain huts. The Nuvolao was built in 1883; then came the von Glanwell in the Travenanzes valley in 1886, today's Vandelli on the Sorapis near the little "magic" lake in 1901, one year before the Pal-

mieri at the foot of Croda da Lago. It was precisely at the end of the nineteeth century that, influenced by foreign alpinistic tourism, Lady Potts and her friend Lady Bury, deeply in love with the Ampezzo valley, arranged for the construction of a romantic villa in the neo-gothic style which became the setting for society parties and suggestive hunting outings. What's more, in honor of their love for hunting, the villa took up the name of Sant'Hubertus, the patron saint of hunters. The two Englishladies obtained a concession over a vast territory between the Tofane and the Badia Valley (corresponding to part of today's Natural Park), where they organized enthusiastic chamois shooting parties together with their noble and sophisticated guests.
Sant'Hubertus villa rose near the historic ruins of the Bottestagno Castle, a suggestive reference point for those arriving on foot from the Badia Valley, through Fanes or the Fodara plateau, or for those arriving from Dobbiaco by coach.

Unfortunately, during the Second World War a bomb tore down the fairy-tale building, turning it into a heap of stones; this, however, can but add further charm to the area, passing on to the curious tourist the surprise and enchantment of past epoques of which only imagination gives evidence.

The Great War interrupted the growth of tourism in Cortina which, as of the beginning of the century, was being visited by the pioneers of skiing during wintertime. The new road from Falzarego, connecting it to Bolzano, was inaugurated in August 1909 and had been created for tourist purposes, though it certainly concealed quite different aims for the Austrians who perceived the possibility of war breaking out with the Italians.
Death and destruction, of which the Cortina mountains and many Ampezzo dwellers were sad witnesses or leading actors, was followed by recovery - once more urged by the unsuppressable cry of the peaks. Emilio

Comici climbed the Civetta, the Spigolo Giallo of Lavaredo and, together with the brothers Angelo and Giuseppe Dimai, the northern face of the greater Lavaredo (1933). The exploits of Riccardo Cassin and of many other Italian, Austrian and German alpinists followed suit, as well as the foundation, in 1939, of the Scoiattoli Society, created by strong young Ampezzo climbers, their activity still being

widely renowned.
At the same time, society life in Cortina grew with the visits of not only mountain lovers or aristocratic European families or, again, small unique cultural circles attended by men such as Filippo De Pisis, Dino Buzzati, Goffredo Parise. Over those years and after the Second World War, over a period of time that reaches present days, Cortina has dressed the glittering colors of fashion and of the most sophisticated taste trends, identifying itself in places and meeting routes that have already become famous because visited by thousands of faces - known, less known or even unknown - that belong to the world of cinema, of shows and of illustrated magazines or to the wealthiest and most prestigious sets of society.

But, next to this cream world and, at times, interlocked with it, are all those who love Cortina for its meadows and woods, for its silent stones and swirling waters. The valley offers a vast choice of promenades, more or less demanding, more or less lonely, of "iron" trails at all levels which, except during "rush weeks", preserve that feeling of peacefulness and calm that only the most remote corners can arouse. It is not rare to spot, in this triumph of wild nature, shy marmots, chamois, squirrels and foxes that have finally resumed ownership over their territory. Like them, many people feel that only when the tourist flow is scarse can it become possible to re-establish a contact point between man and nature, can nature itself resume its dimension in man's heart. Only when it is far away from human sounds can the

silence of nature be filled with its languages and reconquer its original vocation - a unique one -, filling the hearts of those who deeply feel it, thus finally closing a circle which, without it, would remain incomplete.

In such a beautiful area, Cortina's fate had already been marked. The great cult of the land on the part of those living on it, however, has protected the valley from all the traps that tourist development harbors.

Independent of the 1980's ideas of ecology or environmental protection, the spirit underlying the safeguard of Cortina has much deeper roots. It has to do with lifestyle and a way of conceiving nature as the element that has permitted life to continue for over two thousand years. Therefore, it is an act of acknowledgement rather than a political or fashion trend. Hence, the construction of new houses is strictly regulated, also in terms of style and external features: the typological characteristics of the buildings must refer to the typical Ampezzo architecture.

105 THE VAST AMPEZZO VALLEY.

Initially it was the mightiest mountain, the peak that mostly attracted alpinists; then, the less important but still inviolated peaks were reached.

It was then the turn of the more logical routes, in search for natural and smooth ascents; then, it was the search for demanding routes. Finally, the spasmodic hunt for the challenge put forth by routes that were at the limit of one's means. Climbing techniques have evolved with the same rhythm as has route selection. In the beginning, it was the "guide", the customer and a safety rope between the two. Then came spikes, used only to overcome the most demanding passages.

Then it was the turn of spiked routes from the fastening point to the peak. Today, in some way, the technique is going backwards: spikes only for safety, but the climb should be done absolutely "freely". Modern equipment, such as superadherent shoes, a more intense athletic preparation and a new notion of climbing make it possible to achieve results and levels that only a few years ago were unthinkable.

106 Tools belonging to an old "Guide".

107 An easy climb.

108 Tanning at 3000 meters.

109 A difficult "free-climbing".

The rock-climbing training grounds are faces dedicated to climbing exercises: instead of venturing in long climbs on high mountains, climbers can alternate different and shorter routes, all on the same rock.
Cinque Torri are considered rock climbers' paradise, as they offer wide ranges of difficulties, degrees and levels. The area is near the road to Falzarego, easily reachable on foot: it is a thirty-minute walk among firs and larches, along the road leading to the old Rifugio Cinque Torri. This environment baptized the debut of thousands of rock-climbers, thus harboring the atmosphere of moments and emotions which, despite the going by of time, are always the same.
Modern Rifugio Scoiattoli is completely different and can be reached by chair-lift or on foot, climbing up the ski slope. Its name comes from the group of expert Ampezzo rock-climbers that was set up way back in 1939.

111 YOUNG ROCK-CLIMBERS.

110 "DOUBLE-ROPE" DESCENT AT THE CINQUE TORRI.

112 "IRON" TRAIL TO PUNTA ANNA.

Thanks to the "iron" trails, it is now possible to follow routes that otherwise would too demanding, and reach peaks, places and faces of rare beauty and grand sight. For example, from the Lorenzi mountain hut on the Cristallo mountain (photo 115), the Ivano Dibona "iron" trail (photo 116) leads to Ospitale. The "iron" trail, of average difficulty, starts off on a plank bridge suspended in the air (photo 117) and runs along the ridges of the Cristallo group: Creste Bianche, Vecio del Forame, Zurlon, Col dei Stombe. The route is an extremely panoramic one, as it runs along the chain separating the Cortina valley from the Carbonin valley in direction of Dobbiaco. Moreover, it is particularly interesting because it unwinds in the sites where many battles were fought during the First World War; evidence of these are the remains of camps, trenches and galleries. Leaving the most demanding part, the one on the rock-face, one can stroll down to the suggestive Val Padeon, the depression separating the Cristallo group from the Pomagagnon group. Meadows and an ideal inclination, also for mountain biking, are a relief after the efforts made on the "iron" trail, up to the Ospitale mountain hut, served by bus rides on the Cortina-Dobbiaco main road.

116 BRIDGES AND GALLERIES OF THE FIRST WORLD WAR.

117 THE SUSPENSION BRIDGE ALONG THE "IVANO DIBONA" TRAIL.

113 HIKERS ALONG AN "IRON" TRAIL.

114 AN "IRON" TRAIL TO CRESTE BIANCHE.

115 RIFUGIO LORENZI AT STAUNIES.

118 THE STEEP GORGE ALONG THE "MARINO BIANCHI" TRAIL.

There are various "iron" trails on the Tofane, one for every taste and degree of experience.

In the front section, starting from the Pomedes mountain hut, is the "iron" trail called Punta Anna (photo 120), which climbs up along the lower rocks of Tofana di Mezzo, with even quite exposed tracts. Towards the end, the "iron" trail runs parallel to the Cableway, the Freccia nel Cielo (Arrow in the Sky), undoubtedly a less tiring alternative route to the peak. The entire charm of Tofana di Rozes can be enjoyed along the Lipella "iron" trail. Starting from the Castelletto gallery, full of war findings, the trail runs around the mountain, parallel to spectacular Val Travenanzes, and reaches a ridge called Tre Dita (Three Fingers). From here alpinists can continue towards the peak or descend along the typical slanted slabs to the Giussani mountain hut and, from here, follow the scree to Dibona, were a glass of beer and a sandwich will reward every effort. Even to the unexperienced alpinists the Astaldi and Olivieri trails offer unknown and unrisky emotions.

119 AN "IRON" TRAIL.

120 THE "IRON" TRAIL TO TOFANA DI MEZZO (VIA MACKINTOSH).

Eyes roam endlessly and hearts are filled with an unterrable feeling of infinity. Who can resist such a sight? Peaks following other peaks in an atmosphere rarified by height, in the light of an unprecedented flashing of the sun, in the reflection of the stones that seem to be as white as snow, in the uncatchable evaporation of the clouds. Moreover, what strikes is the extension and calm of the landscape, barren but intact, along the ascent towards the peak of Croda del Becco (photo 121).

It is the area of summer mountain grazing, chosen, not by chance, because of its abundance of meadows and spring water.

This is where the Boite stream rises, running down the entire Cadore valley, to then flow into the Piave River. The gentle slopes seem to concentrate around the old summer hut of Ra Stua, today a pleasant rest area for hikers, who can start off from here to follow routes leading to the Fodara Vedla plain or to Val Salata (Salted Valley), towards the Sennes mountain hut, or climb among dwarf pines to the Biella mountain hut.

121   THE SMALL BIELLA MOUNTAIN HUT VIEWED FROM CRODA DEL BECCO.

In August, many trails are used intensively by summer tourists and hikes are often interrupted by greetings and expected and unexpected meetings. An almost obligatory route is the walk from the Tre Croci Pass to Rifugio Vandelli with its spectacular lake; the double route passing Croda da Lago to the Palmieri mountain hut, crossing the woody climb from the Giau road, or along the easier trail coming from Lake Ajal; or, still, the walk to the peak of Mount Nuvolao, with its omonimous mountain hut. Those who prefer less crowded and more silent areas, however, may choose from a vast range of marked trails, though not so popular, such as those of Valle d'Antruiles, or trail n. 0 leading to the Dall'Oglio bivouac, or the Lerosa plateau and the Alpe di Fosses. But it is in autumn that the magic of colors, together with the intact quietness of the mountain, make the routes even more suggestive and fascinating, thus actually conquering the hearts of real Ampezzo-lovers. Then, the silent vastness of the landscapes highlights details that are tiny but also unique, as they have never been noticed before.

122 THE CRUCIFIX AT 2780 METERS ON THE LAGAZUOI.

123 THE NUVOLAO MOUNTAIN HUT.

124 ON CRESTE BIANCHE.

125 AN EASY WALK ON ALPE DI LEROSA.

126 A 1915-18 WAR MEMORIAL CRUCIFIX.

For those who do not love arduous hikes, or for simple leisurely-ramblers, there are faster ways of climbing the steep slopes of the mountains surrounding Cortina and nevertheless enjoy the view. The arrival terraces of the valley cableways are also famous as mountain sun-bathing sites, both in summer and in winter. Nevertheless, besides listening to the music coming from your walkman, or reading your bestseller or chatting with friends, you can admire one of the most spectacular views of the entire Dolomites.

127 THE SIGHT OFFERED FROM TOFANA DI MEZZO.

128 THE LAST JUMP OF THE "FRECCIA NEL CIELO" TOWARDS THE TOFANA.

The cableway to Monte Faloria was the second one to be constructed in the Ampezzo valley and it links Cortina directly to the alpine pole of the Faloria and the Sorapis. Up high, fast chair-lifts quickly churn out the flow of escursionists even in "peak" periods, while warm alpine huts and enormous sunny terraces offer the possibility of having a pleasant rest.

The spectacular view that one commands from the peak of Monte Lagazuoi is even more exciting when seen from inside the cableway (photos 131 - 132) linking, with no intermediate pillars, the Falzarego Pass station to the arrival station at 2756 meters of height. This cableway functions quite a lot both in winter and in summer: the long slope on the front face of the mountain allows for sunny descents while, in the summertime, there are many routes starting off from here and leading to some of the most beautiful spots in the area. Val Travenanzes starts from the Lagazuoi; it is a marvellous uninhabited valley running behind the Tofane group, reaching Ponte Alto and, from there, to Fiames.

129 EDELWEISSES.

130 THE SON FORCA CHAIR-LIFT.

131 ARRIVAL STATION OF THE CABLEWAY TO MOUNT LAGAZUOI.

132 CABLEWAYS IN THE FOG.

In the evening, Cortina changes into an enormous glittering living-room, where famous and unknown figures stroll, in the most absolute elegance, glad that they can participate in customs that have become actual rites.
In those periods of heavy tourist flow, tea and sweets at Lovat's or kraphen at Embassy's are a must between one "downtown stroll" and another on Corso Italia.

133 THE HISTORIC "COPPA D'ORO".

135 LUNCH AT RA STUA.

134 "DOUBLE ROPE" DESCENT FROM THE BELL-TOWER.

136 PROMENADE DOWN THE MAIN STREET.

Having bought chocolates at Zestel's, sunglasses at Zardini's, fabrics at Moessmer's, sweatshirts at Meeting's, and after the daily promenade down the colorful ailes of the Cooperativa, almost as if in a modern museum, the time is right for an aperitif at the elegant Hotel de la Poste, or for a glass of prestigious wine at Jerry's tiny wine bar which, just like Mary Poppins' bag, manages always to find a seat for everyone.
Cortina also has a less futile and more committing face: its art exhibitions, conferences, literature happenings are really of great cultural interest.

137   THE WHITE STONE BELL-TOWER THAT HAS NOW BECOME THE SYMBOL OF CORTINA.

THE TRADITIONS

SO OLD AND DEEPLY-ROOTED IN THEIR WHOLENESS.

In the quiet world of Ampezzo, the days, months, seasons of nature and life, meetings, thoughts and aspirations of entire generations have merged and developed according to rhythms and manners that have been repeated entirely in time, thus making up that heritage of precious customs and traditions that we know so well. A legacy that has managed to be handed down to today - despite profound social and economic changes and independently of all complex customs changes - thanks to the spirit and wisdom of the Ampezzo people who have learned to treasure their past and the vital energy of their forefathers. Ever since the darkest and most distant centuries, the dwellers have learned - with toil, enrichment of experiences, joy and sorrow - to face the thousands of problems linked to survival, when the woods took land away from pastures and agriculture, when the frozen snow of long winters halted the course of life, when the boulders sliding off the mountains rolled down to the valley, dragging along mud and uprooted trees. In time, this concrete meaning of existence has become religious feeling and has taken root in a profound christian faith that is inexorably linked to daily acts, to the rhythm of the seasons and of the work activities, to the occuring of important events. For example, the feast that is celebrated on January 19th in remembrance of the miraculous intervention of the Madonna who, according to the legend, protected the Ampezzo dwellers from a Gothic assault, shrouding the enemies in a mantle of clouds, thus leading them to kill each other. Though lacking historical evidence, this remembrance has reached present times in a mixture of superstition and christianity, sealed by the successive construction of the church dedicated to the Defending Madonna. Today, despite the inevitable stimulations that tourism hosts, it is still customary to celebrate also the feast of Our Lady of the Assumption on the evening of August 14th, at the time of the summer harvest, when enormous bonfires are lit in the valley and on the surrounding hills to light up the spreading darkness of the sky. Likewise, the tradition of processions is kept alive, such as those for the Corpus Domini and the Holy Rosary, when the statue of the Madonna that is preserved on the altar constructed by Brustolon in the parish church of S.S. Filippo e Giacomo, is lifted and carried down the village streets, in the midst of traditional banners. Many other festivity traditions have instead disappeared as of today: the ways of praying, the past pilgrimages (on foot to Santa Maria Luggau, for

example), the "rogations", which were processions from one chapel to another covering the entire valley to obtain from God the favor of clear skies during harvest time, have all been lost because religiousness and relationships with nature today occupy a different position in everday life. Yet, remembering the old country beliefs that were based on watching all natural events and their surprising interlocking, maintains an equally surprising charm on us, a charm that, perhaps, is aroused by an innate inclination to return to our origins: the influence of lunar phases on agricultural activites, on woodcutting, on meadow mowing, on clothes washing and on animal breeding has always attracted our imagination; we keep believing in those signs coming from the sky that tradition alone has managed to change

into significant ones. The Ampezzo people's wisdom and faith in the future and in life have been consolidated over the centuries, thanks to the retrieval of a profound and concrete sense of community solidarity; from the common management of pastures and woods on the basis of the Regole principles, it has crept into individual acquaintances, in the relationship between neighbors, in the actions aiming at facing natural calamities. In fact, neighbors had the task of supporting mourning families, caring for the deceased and the house in times of sorrow, granting hospitality in their homes in case of fires, of-

fering their help in fieldwork and wood-cutting.

After all, the community spirit of the Ampezzo people has always been reflected in the typical organization of their living settlements which have always developed in huddled clusters of houses, normally one-family buildings, near areas that were mostly favorable to agricultural activities.

In each of these "villages" around the center of Cortina (which was considered as such because of its parish church and cemetery), there was a common fountain for drinking water drawing, for animal watering and clothes washing. Then, with time, a small church was erected, to make the life of every single community more complete. The typical Ampezzo dwelling gathered all family needs into one single, compact building: the front looked southwards and was made of stones; it was used as living quarters. The back, made of wood, was used as stable and the barn, called "toulà", was on top of it. Today such barns are considered precious carpentry creations: while the parapets of the older balconies were only made up of simple upright wooden planks set one next to the other, in the Nineteenth century, thanks also to the influence of the local art school, terraces were enriched by finely carved railings.

Inside the living area, on the right of the entrance, was the "stua", the heart of the house itself. It was a room that was completely lined with wood and equipped with a dome-shaped stove, the plaster-walled "el fornèl". Above the dome was a wooden structure where the children and the old sat in its warmth. The family gathered in the "stua" after a day of work to chat, to carry out household chores and to say the daily rosary.

Next to the "stua" was the kitchen with its "larin", an open hearth that was normally built against a wall, where food was cooked. The bedrooms normally were on the first floor.

The Ampezzo people's diet was poor and simple, based on the moderate consumption of the fruits that the land yielded after hard work and of the few products com-ing from their animals. Milk was used to produce butter, cheese, "ricotta", that was then smoked on the "larin". Meat, also smoked and normally sheep meat, was eaten only on Sundays, cut into small chunks and added to barley or fava bean soup.

On holidays or important occasions, typical dishes were prepared, many of which are still widespread and well-known, such as "casunziei", half-moon-shaped ravioli with a mixture of red beetroots and potatoes or field herbs filling, or "carafoi", deep-fried puff-pastry cakes. Food was seasoned with pork and sheep fat, preserved in salt, pepper, sage leaves, laurel leaves and juniper berries. Honey was used instead of sugar. Bread was home-baked until last century, when Massimiliano Apollonio introduced the custom of using a mixture of rye, barley and fava bean flour supplied by every family to make the bread that he would bake in his home oven - today's Hotel Concordia. The amount of time spent working was long and tiring. By means of their agricultural activities, the Ampezzo people produced all they needed to survive. The few tillable areas were planted with cereals (barley, oats and wheat), fava beans and, as of the beginning of the Twentieth Century, also potatoes. Flax, too, was tilled and the women then spun it at home to make linen. The vast meadows climbing up to the first rocks were used to gather hay for herdfeeding. Men and women worked together right from the early morning sunrays, cutting grass and spreading it out to dry, often worrying over the darkening sky covered with rainthreatening clouds that would have made every effort vain. Hay harvesting, like felling, was governed by the strict rules of the Regole. Every family had its own work tools, marked by a special brand, the "segn de ciasa", that was used also to mark all timber employed for the construction of the family house.

The sheep, instead, were taken to the high pastures during the summer by an Ampezzo dweller who was chosen every year by the Regole community; the sheep were marked with different cuts on their ears, "rà noda", to facilitate identification and their belonging to one family or the other.

To distinguish the many families having the same surname, nicknames were used on the basis of a person's physical and expressive traits, or on the basis of his job or of the most peculiar episodes in his life, a life that, after all, was marked by a customary and homogeneous rhythm which, in time, became tradition. Therefore, just like the cycle of agricultural activities was inexorably repeated as seasons appeared, the existance of men and women also evolved, in their quest for feelings, in the blooming of love, in the joy of motherhood, in the fulfilment of thought.

Marriage, a particular and definite event, was preceded and/or accompanied - in its evolution - by a complicated series of rituals, charged with conscious and profound meaning: the "zesto" ceremony, one week before the event. It was a meal offered in the bride's home, during which the parents agreed upon the number of guests and their mutual responsibilities. The name of the ceremony comes from the basket that was used to hold the gifts the spouses gave each other and those that they received from their witnesses. Normally, the groom's gift to his future wife would be the apron for her formal dress, while her gift to him was a white shirt.

The witness's gift to the bride would be her wedding ring and sometimes a hairpin in the shape of a dove holding a precious stone, a heart and an arrow in its beak, respectively the symbols of savings, love and the straight and narrow path. The groom's walk to the church on the wedding day was interrupted in every neighborhood by friends and relatives doing the socalled "stanga", forcing him to imitate some trade, nor-

mally having to do with his job, and to pay his friends a toll.

Like many others, this custom is still alive, as if to give today's world evidence of the fact that the Ampezzo valley traditions are not merely part of recollections, but are still alive in everyone's heart, contributing to the formation of everyone's personality, just as genetic heredities do.

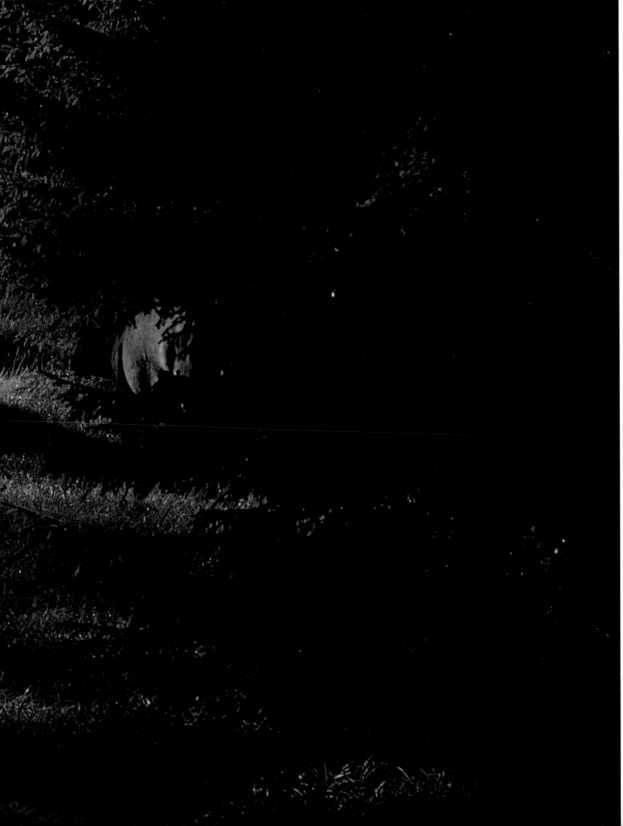

Cortina has not forgotten its shepherd roots completely. In the more intimate dimension of low season, the last signs of authentic rural life can still be witnessed: the life that should not be shown to everyone, or about which nothing is absolutely necessary to be told. The difference with the peak season is really deep. At times it even seems impossible to bridge. After the long period of summer mountain grazing, the cattle return to the villages. Actually, when hiking, they are rarely seen. Of course, this is because they are not so numerous anymore, but also because the areas used for summer grazing are slightly off the most beaten tracks.

143 S.S. Trinità in Maion.

Although an actually Ampezzo architectural typology does not exist, there are many features that are common to all the valley buildings. The brickwork, used as living quarters, is always on the front part of the house, while in the back is the barn, made completely of wood.

Every family had its personal mark on all its firewood, timber, work tools, etc. The "segno di casa" (house mark) (photo 145), as it was called, was passed on from father to son. In case the family was divided by two sons, one of these kept the original mark while the other added a small stroke to it. This tradition is so deeply rooted that there is a book of marks (photo 146) bearing all the marks and relating them to their respective families.

145   A HOUSE MARK (1600).

146   THE BOOK OF MARKS.

147   FARMHOUSE DATED 1600.

144   AN OLD BARN.

148   TYPICAL AMPEZZO BUILDING (1700).

No old Ampezzo home is without a "stua", the entirely pine wood-lined room where families spent most of their free time.
There was a reason for this: it was the only heated room.
The "stua" was often the householder's "masterpiece" and he would decorate it with capitals, embellishments and the "campo", a ceiling rose.
The "stua" normally had very few pieces of furniture: a square table with a bench around it, a corner cupboard, a multicolored carpet; everything was characterized by absolute simplicity.

149 INSIDE A FARMHOUSE. THE "STUA".

150 LATE LIGHTS LIGHTLY CARRESS THE DWELLINGS.

In the past, sheep were fundamental to survival; today they have been drastically reduced in number because of the changes in the valley's economy.
The custom of summer mountain grazing was determined by the fact that low pastures were entirely available for agriculture and hay-making.
Normally, on October 4th, the sheep return to the bottom of the valley. It is an extremely exciting and suggestive sight: the single man responsible for summer grazing takes the sheep to a site where the families can recognize them (photo 152) on the basis of a mark called "noda" that is cut on

151 THE BOOK OF MARKS.

152 SHEEP DIVISIO.

153 SHEEP SHEARING.

154 SHEEP RETURNING TO THE VILLAGE.

155 LAST GRAZINGS BEFORE WINTER.

their ears. In this case too, there is a book that is still being used and that contains records of such marks (photo 151). According to a centuries-old custom, every spring, a person responsible for the sheep is chosen among the "regolieri" and he cannot refuse this assignment. He normally reaches the grazing areas every two days to check that no heads are missing. Summer mountain huts were used by sheperds to milk cows and then make butter, cheese and "ricotta".

156 FODARA VEDLA.

157 SHEEP AT ALVERÀ.

158 A STABLE IN COL.

The Cortina bell-tower is the reference point, almost a symbol, of the entire valley.
No matter from what viewpoint it is observed, it appears splendid - not so much for its artistic features which are, actually, not so special - but for its whiteness, its constant presence, its protective aura. It can be seen in modern postcards, just as it was pictured in those of the past century, now collection pieces. And again: those who lie down to rest on a meadow or wander in the woods or down the grassy slopes around town and cannot spot its white soaring profile, can nevertheless hear its tolls beating the hours and days, one after the other, with that simplicity that makes one really feel at home. Till the end of the nineteenth century, the Municipality had established a special activity: a person was appointed to climb up to the bell cell every night at set intervals and, from here, carefully watch the whole village in search of any sign of fire: in a village made up of predominantly wooden houses and barns full of hay, a fire would have soon involved the entire neighborhood. In case of fire, he was to warn the inhabitants immediately by ringing a bell that was reserved exclusively for this type of emergency.

159 THE BELL-TOWER.

160 THE CLOCK.

161 THE BIG BELL.

162 THE CHURCH AT SUNDOWN.

163 The dwellings of Campo di Sopra and the narrow road to Cortina.

What best can tell about a person's lifestyle if not the clothes he is wearing? Today the Ampezzo costumes are worn in Cortina only on special occasions, during town feasts or weddings; but until the beginning of this century, they were men and women's normal everyday clothes.

Or rather, there was an everyday version and a special occasion one. What can normally be seen today is the "ra magnes", the outfit that was worn on feast-days, on wedding days and even on one's own wedding day. It was a long black curly skirt - it was eventually shortened to mid-calf length -, sewn unto a bodice of the same color and from which a silk scarf came out. Then there was a small black jacket opened in the front and a silk apron, "el palegren", normally with flowery motifs matching the scarf and which was as long as the skirt.

As of the beginning of the nineteenth century, it became customary to embellish the traditional black hat, unto which black ribbons were already sewn, with black ostrich feathers. Maybe this female coquetry was the result of the influence of the new English tourism that spread all over Cortina at that particular time.

If a woman was married, she could decorate the scarf coming out of the bodice with a red, light-blue or pink silk ribbon matching her apron, and even replace the silk material with embroidered tulle. It was absolutely forbidden to use the "drapo de ra cordela infizada" before the wedding day.

164 A LITTLE GIRL (OIL PAINTING DATED 1850).

165 "RA MAGNES", THE IMPORTANT COSTUME.

166 THE CORTINA MUSICAL ENSEMBLE FOUNDED IN 1863.

The "ciamesoto" was an ever-present element in all Ampezzo costumes, even in the winter one and everyday clothing, the "ra jaida".
Suffice it to add two black sleeves and to cover it with a very serious black bodice buttoned up in front. The apron was made of more common and heavy material, normally striped; a soft square boucle' woolen shawl was worn on top of it. Today the musicians wear the so-called "a ra vecia", a costume which fell into disuse at the end of the eighteenth century. During summertime, the outfit was always the "ra varnàza", whether or not it was a holiday. The "ciamesòto" remained but the bodice had white curly sleeves and the shawl was colored - obviously matching the apron - and was made of silk or cotton, depending on the occasion. Men dressed in a very simple manner, using home-made fabrics. On the occasion of ceremonies, some would wear a short jacket with half belt over a white shirt and a damasked vest; a small silk scarf was used as a tie and was pinned down by a golden or silver tiepin.

167 GIRL'S COSTUME.

168 READY FOR THE PARADE.

169 COSTUME, DETAIL.

170 MALE COSTUME.

171 A HORSEMAN CARRYING THE CORTINA BANNER.

Until the end of last century, when agricultural activities still guaranteed subsistance to the Ampezzo dwellers, the extension and growth of woods were kept under control: toil and hard work were necessary to uproot and remove trees and stones to allow cereals and pulses to be cropped and meadows to be prepared for haying down lower, near the bottom of the valley; whereas higher up, room was made for summer livestock grazing and simple wooden fences were built around pastures.

173 FELLING IN VALBONA.

The land and the fruits it yielded were the life itself of the Ampezzo dwellers who, eversince the most ancient times, codified the Laudi of the Regole - a system aiming at the common safeguard and exploitation of woods and pastures. The woodcutter's trade was matched by that of the hammerman who had the task of marking the trees and dividing them according to their age and diameter. Only a few of these, those with the right number of years, were then felled by the woodcutters. Thus, it was certain that every year a certain number of trees could be felled and the woods could continue to grow and expand as envisaged. This type of "census" still continues existing and, in autumn, one can often see trees bearing the "hammerman's" mark.

174 HAY MANTLE.

175 THE SUMMER MOUNTAIN HUT OF FEDERA.

The religiousness of the Ampezzo dwellers has profound and ancient roots. In the past it materialized - certainly more than today - in traditional rites, community prayer, the variety of ceremonies linking everyone's daily life - with his needs and wants, his joys and sorrows - to the sublime entity of the Divine.

There was certainly a greater compenetration between life outside the church doors and life in church, also thanks to the lacking self-confidence that man then had - less faith in progress and in the power of money.

The Ampezzo dwellers still maintain enormous religiousness, like do many of the religious traditions that have been handed down for centuries.

The eve of the Assumption, for example - at the time of propitiating good haying - is still celebrated by lighting enormous bonfires all over the valley, up to the mountain ridges, and in the light and warmth of these fires the people dance, sing, drink and eat. Today like in the past.

176 THE BAROQUE ALTAR OF THE "BEATA VERGINE DELLA DIFESA".

177 THE "PARISH CHURCH".

178 THE CORPUS DOMINI PROCESSION.

179 "OUT OF MASS", OIL PAINTING BY G. GHEDINA DATED 1860.

It is narrated that the Madonna della Difesa was erected in remembrance of a miracle that the Virgin Mary made at the time of the Goths. During an invasion of these barbarians, She allegedly made such thick fog fall on the enemy camp - today's borough of Lacedel which probably got its name from the spears used in the past - , that they lost their sense of direction completely and killed each other. The Goth Madonna is still celebrated with a procession which every year on January 19 starts from the "Difesa" - as the Ampezzo dwellers call the church - and unwinds along the town streets.

180 Madonna dei Battuti.

181 Putto. Work by Andrea Brustolon (1662 - 1737).

Despite its being the only one in the Dolomites that is made of white stones, the Cortina bell-tower is perfectly integrated in the landscape. Perhaps it is precisely its whiteness that reflects so well the colors of every instant of the day - that absorbs them, filters them and then reflects them in perfect symbiosis.

It is almost as if it wanted to stress the fundamental role it plays at every moment of the day in the valley. It is the unquestioned leading actor in everyone's day and hour, the beloved protector of the valley. To think that the "new" bell-tower was built only in mid-1800, when the old one started "falling to pieces", jeopardizing the lives of passer-bys. In a few years it was designed, examined, approved and constructed.

And now it is so well integrated in the surrounding environment that no one would even think of doubting its eternal existence, before the first house in Cortina was built. Perhaps it was because of this bell-tower that the town grew precisely around this borough.

182 SYMPHONIC ORCHESTRA CONCERT IN THE PARISH CHURCH.

183 The bell-tower profile against the lit faces of the Faloria.

Autumn is still the calmest season in Cortina. Summer tourists have left, the days grow shorter, colors die down at first, to then explode in the thousands of yellow and red hues. The woods actually seem pictures that have been painted in such an artistic manner as nature alone is capable of doing.

They fill one's sight and, although lacking the enormous summer sun that warms up the air, the warmth of the colors of the trees changes the grayness of the autumn days into a triumphant fire.

Such colors, already so varying according to the type of tree wearing them, manage to change again according to the sun inclination, thus offering ever-changing sights, now gold now red, removing all shadows of monotony from what - in theory - should be the most monotonous season.

184 WORK TOOLS.

185 CORTINA IN THE GOLDEN COLORS OF OCTOBER.

One is probably influenced by the surrounding landscape also in his vocations and aspirations.
The extraordinary beauty of the Cortina mountains, of the green meadows and autumn-colored woods must have made the Ampezzo dwellers' eyes used to seeing painting-like sights.
Cortina's artistic tradition is deeply rooted in the most ancient past and legends, such as the one about a strange woman-painter who lived in a cave on the Faloria, go hand in hand with unconfirmed "rumours" maintaining that Tiziano was born in a house in Campo di Sotto.
The Ghedina brothers frescoed the old drugstore with images picturing

186 FRESCO IN MELERES.

various moments in life, because in Cortina every moment is worth a painting.

Are the Ampezzo dwellers in their traditional costumes not good painting subjects or, again, the autumn landscapes with the pink mountains looming against the blue sky? Or the fir-trees, pine trees, larches loaded with snow in a fairy tale setting?

187 DETAIL OF THE OLD DRUGSTORE FRESCOED BY G. GEDINA.

188 WAITING FOR THE PARADE.

Just like a precious stone laid in the gold of a bright jewel, Cortina shines in its valley. Protected by the arch of mountains surrounding it, with its extremely narrow and almost unaccessible southward opening, Cortina has never become an important trade or crossroad area. On one hand this has penalized all possible productive vocations but, on the other, it has been useful in preserving local beauty. Tourism has become the Ampezzo dwellers' main activity and for this reason, although to the detriment of other old crafts, it has contributed to enhance the preciousness of the valley. Historically, no great superpower - under whose direct control Cortina often was - has ever managed to impose its sway on the Ampezzo people because, thanks to their independent character, the latter have always maintained a high degree of autonomy; likewise, progress, which has changed the face of most of Italy profoundly, was particularly light-handed when handling the valley of Cortina. Perhaps it was because the unique nature of this resort area, the perfect balancing of its elements, the preciousness of its details, the grand mightiness of its rocks were all fully understood and this defended, as if in a casket, the integrity of this priceless jewel.

189 CRODA DEL BECCO CLOSES THE VALLEY.

THE SNOW

THE SEASON IN WHICH CORTINA CHANGES.

When Cortina wears its white blanket, it changes completely not only in its aspect but also in its personality and becomes as lively as ever, so busy as it is with all its white activities. It is the most sports- and society-life aspect of Cortina. What in the past used to be a period of lethargy, when people remained indoors near their stoves warming up their hearts and frozen bones with family talks, or in the barns repairing tools, today is, instead, the most lively moment in the entire Ampezzo year. The season opens, in general, on the day of the Immaculate Conception: on December 8th, when the skiing lifts, after having been well oiled and tested after the summer rest, start up again to stop only at Easter or even later. Ski-lovers, who never miss their appointment with the opening of the season, excitedly reach Cortina after the long period of forced inactivity, to try out the beautiful Cortina slopes, to check out any new changes in the lifts or slopes, to "see" if this year the bed is "good" and if, therefore, the season forecasts shall be more or less favorable. It will then be up to the sky to satisfy their expectancies and make their dream of having two meters of snow everywhere come true ...

Once the forecasting survey is through, the sportsmen go back

to the city, anxiously awaiting Christmas holidays, or the typical one-week skiing holiday in February or March.

Christmas is the period of the year in which society life undoubtedly rules out mountain life. Cortina hosts famous names of people in the public eye, of people belonging to nobilities of all times. The "downtown promenade" along Corso Italia around six o'clock p.m. is a "must", even more than the daily downhill run is. Furcoats, fantastic mises and soaring purchases for the ladies; parties and dinner parties to be organized or to attend for ladies and gentlemen; discoes and New Year's Eve parties for young ones; chats and gossips for everyone.

The atmosphere is extremely lively with sparkling voices and so much desire for entertainment. It looks like a fairy world, so distant from everyone's everyday city life, so cheerful and sumptuous ... The Cortina Cooperativa is so crowded that it becomes inaccessible during rush hours and one cannot tell whether it is a luxury department store, a delicatessen supermarket or a meeting place. The tables in the most famous restaurants are reserved already in September, not to mention the tables at Jerry's Wine Bar, that tiny bar that reminds us of Mary Poppins' bag for the number of persons it manages to host.

And there is a big advantage also for those who do not agree with this atmosphere of fashionable Cortina: since the "downtown promenades" are more popular than skiing, the ski slopes are not particularly crowded, especially early in the morning when the previous night's follies induce many to prefer the white of the bed to that of

the slopes. Those who love skiing and plunging deep into nature can have their fill of the marvellous December snow and clear mountain sky and then, as it grows dark, they let the bottom of the valley enchant them as they admire it, already dark, full of lights at the windows, while the sky is still clear and here and there the rocks are lit up by the setting sun.

During the entire month of January, Cortina passes from the absolute stillness of week days, with their normal working life, to the sudden week-end crowding up, which the fondest of them - often owners of a season ski pass - never give up.

Here, the 160 kilometers of ski slopes and the many, although not futuristic, ski lifts can make a fine showing. Although length is not the best feature of the Cortina ski slopes, their pride lies in their beauty, both in terms of panorama and of technical characteristics. They are slopes with a noble past, perhaps even an olympic one, rich in traditions and with an almost mythical aura. Famous personages and important public figures have skied down the Cortina slopes. Amongst the early skiers descending the Procol and the Tofane were the Romanovs, King Hubert and the entire Royal Family, the Duke of Aosta and Leon Tolstoji as a spectator, but also all those advocators of winter tourism in Ampezzo who are important Italian figures today.

Besides the famous sportsmen of the Fifties who brought as much honor to Cortina as do today's superb champions, Ilio Colli, after whom a slope is also named, Bruno Alberti, Giovanni Dibona, and today Kristian Ghe-

dina, are all names that Ampezzo is proud of. The Tofana ski slopes, which many will remember unprepared for skiing and covered with humps, have now been widened to host the increasing flow of sportsmen arriving in search of technical crossings and difficulties. The yellow headlights and blinking lights of the snowcats can be seen in the middle of the night as they prepare the "Canalone" or

the "Stra", a World Cup slope, for the morrow. Moreover, the artificial snow-making ensures accessibility to such slopes also when not even the most complicated "snow dances" seem to be successful.

Higher up, Ra Valles offers the best snow in the valley - apart from an amazing view - as it lies almost at 3000 meters. A "black" ski slope, for example, is the Forcella Rossa linking the Ra Valles plateau to the other Tofana and Col Druscié ski slopes, and from these, down to the center of Cortina.

Slightly lower, the western pole of the Cortina skiing activities is linked by plants and ski slopes to the Socrepes and Pocol skiing areas, where inexperienced and not necessarily expert skiers can venture upon the "blue" slopes or take lessons from almost

200 ski instructors belonging to the three Cortina ski schools.

On the other flank of the valley, the Faloria and Cristallo lifts system is dedicated mainly to the afternoon sun lovers. When the sunrays are low, the Tondi di Faloria loom up against the sky and scenes can be seen such as those offered in advertising shots, with skiers raising "powdery" snow in the bright blue setting of winter in the mountains (which is bluer than ever). The extension of the Faloria slopes and their variety are an unresistable pole of attraction, also because the fast ski lifts manage to "carry off" even the great Sunday crowds.

Within the reach of everyone, amongst the sunny slopes of the Cristallo, where the great Tomba himself used to practice when he was a young boy, stands out the "blackest black". The verticality of the Staunies gorge strikes a shivering feeling also in the best skiers, maybe also because of the signs which, at the chair-lift departing point, warn that the higher portion of

the slope is reserved to expert skiers. Unfortunately, once at the top, all expectancies are confirmed: in front of the Lorenzi hut there is barely enough room to turn around and, before descending, it is worth stopping - perhaps also to stop shaking in your boots - to look at the view that is really exciting from this spot: snowy peaks endlessly follow one another from the two flanks of the Staunies saddle; the entire Cortina valley can be admired until the Cinque Torri and Lagazuoi ski slopes and one can even see the roundish mightiness of the Marmolada, the highest peak in the Dolomites, whereas on the other side, the Cristallo glacier descends towards Carbonin. All of which is contoured by rocky peaks that can be touched simply by stretching out your arm, and by a pink color that the snow resting on the ridges seems to make even warmer.

In Cortina, ski and nature are an unseparable couple and, even the more so when considering cross-country skiing, the "nordic skiing" of Olympic races: the importance of nature becomes a vital one. From the simpler Fiames ring, with its many length variants, on to the splendid Lake Misurina trail which, rolling over gentle ups and downs, among pines and larches loaded with snow and fascinating white clearings, reaches a trail that runs on the iced surface of the lake, just one step away from the peaks and from the comforts of the hotels.

There are ski slopes for all tastes, many variants to break monotony and, if one really wants, there is also the Cortina-Dobbiaco, as a race or for fun, along the road where the little old mountain train once ran. The trip is made even more mysterious when crossing a tunnel that is lit by dim lightbulbs to cross the spur on which the mythical Bottestagno fort once rose.
Speaking of cross-country skiing, Enrico Colli must be recalled as the Ampezzo dweller who, having to go to Auronzo for a race (30 kilometers from Cor-

tina), left with his skiis on his feet when it was still dark. When he arrived in Auronzo, the race had already started but his stubbornness came off better: without losing heart, he started the race, reached the other racers, passed them and finally won the race.
Like him, Cortina has given the sports-competition world great "names" and, actually, it is still today the Italian municipality which, proportionally to the number of its inhabitants, has supplied the highest number of skiers to the national team.
Suffice it to mention Monti, Siorpaes, Sergio Zardini, Gianfranco Gaspari, Giorgio Alverà who achieved marvellous results in bob-sleighing, holding the Italian colors high also in a specialty that has deeper-rooted traditions abroad. The chute, immersed in the woods, is 1300 meters long, for a run of 55 seconds at average training speed. Thanks to them, also the activity of bob-sleigh production has developed in Cortina: Dandrea "podar" and Siorpaes can boast, in fact, 85% of world pro-

duction, holders as they are of the tiny but important secrets of this "craftsmanship". But Cortina, just like it is at the avanguarde of fashion with its splendid shops, is developing also in

terms of sports. In fact, it is now the seat of an international horse show on snow, an event which, until last year, was held inside the Ice Stadium and is now held on the arrival square of the ski-jump. This brings us to two giants of winter sports that were built for the Olympic Games. Both the Ice Stadium and the Ski-Jump proudly boast the stylistic features of the Fifties, features that have become part

of local nature and still preserve the fascinating glaze of those years, a glaze that is still so fashionable. The latest sporting novelties find good growing grounds in Cortina: it has recently been included in the ring of snow Polo matches which are even more spectacular if plunged in such an extraordinary natural setting. This is the common feature to all winter sports in Cortina: nature has already done a lot in terms of background setting; therefore, human intervention, when creating structures, rather than "doing" something should try to avoid destroying such wonders.

In the past, the snow halted daily chores and all the valley dwellers were left to do was to close themselves indoors and repair broken tools or bake bread; today, the snow is of vital importance to them. Winter tourism, in fact, accounts for a considerable portion of Cortina's activities, as it became an important snow sports area already at the end of last century. Equipped with splendid ski slopes, great hotels - from the luxury hotels to the smaller and more typical ones -, the town hosts a large number of sport-lovers during wintertime. What is particularly appreciated, moreover, is the possibility of having not only the necessary commercial and sporting structures available, but also a suggestive aspect, that aspect that goes directly down to the romantic corner of everyone's heart. Then, the snow turns into something that goes beyond being simply the bed for marvellous skiing: the snow dies down all noises, it makes the atmosphere more intimate and every smile more delicate.

194 ROOFS ARE MADE LIGHTER.

195 SNOWFALL.

196 WINTERTIME VIEWED FROM THE BELL CELL.

106

197 Awakening after a heavy snowfall

198 PIAZZA VENEZIA AND CORSO ITALIA, THE REAL HEART OF CORTINA.

Corso Italia, the real tourist pole of Cortina, fills with passer-bys who, the on the pedestrian area, stop to do their winter shopping. During Christmas holidays the decorated shop windows sparkle with all types of wonderful products. Signed outfits, jewels made by famous artists, leather goods shops and sportswear shops, original and beautiful items, shoes, fabrics, furcoats, and so on.
Cortina really offers everything. The leading position that Cortina occupies in the field of winter sports offers a range of fascinating happenings, also because they are at international level.
The Horse Show on snow, in fact, sees the participation of famous names belonging to the international horse riding scene, on highly potential horses. Cortina also belongs to the circle of Polo games, a sport that is not very popular in Italy but which offers surprising shows both in terms of horsemen and horses, thus attracting world-level jet sets.
The Ice Sculpture Contest (photo 201) is an artistic happening that both adults and children find extremely interesting.

199 POLO ON FROZEN LAKE MISURINA.

200 HORSE SHOW ON SNOW.

201 ICE SCULPTURE.

The Cortina area offers ski-lovers over one hundred and forty kilometers of slopes of every degree, from the small easy runs for beginners to the steeper and technically more difficult ones. The Tofana slope hosts one of the downhill races valid for the World Cup.
In fact, it was the Cortina skiing school that prepared Ampezzoborn Kristian Ghedina, one of the best downhill skiers in the world.
Here, after school, children go skiing and physical education hours are spent taking skiing lessons.
Over two hundred ski instructors belonging to the three Cortina ski schools offer individual and group lessons at all levels.

202 SKIING AT THE TONDI.

203 SKIING AMIDST WOODS AND ROCK-FACES.

204 ALL TOGETHER IN THE CABLEWAY FOR ANOTHER DESCENT.

205 "WORLD CUP RACE" ON THE "OLIMPIA".

Apart from the traditional slopes, from Tondi di Faloria it is possible to slide along the "Vitelli", a natural-type and almost "unlevelled" track that unwinds among little channels, diagonals, jumps and underwood. The descent is easy and satisfying thanks to the continuously spectacular view surrounding the track (photo 206). The emotions that one feels on top of the Tofana (photo 207) are, instead, quite different: leaving your skiis at the Ra Valles station, the high altitude winter scene that one enjoys is breath-taking for its magnificence and is worth the climb.

206 THE "VITELLI" SLOPE AT TONDI DI FALORIA.

207 THE 3224 FROZEN METERS OF THE TOFANA IN WINTERTIME.

208 ICE FALLS.

209 SKIING IN POWDER SNOW.

210 ALONG THE "ARMENTAROLA"

What makes Cortina special is the spectacular sight that one enjoys also from the ski slopes. Infact, they do not run down on rounded-off hilltops, as often happens, but they unwind between the rocks, almost brushing past them. The Forcella Staunies scree is a slope for expert skiers and is literally sunken between two sheer faces while, in front, the entire Ampezzo valley opens up and, to the north, one can spot the valley leading to Dobbiaco.

On the other side of the valley, the Forcella Rossa links Ra Valles, a

plateau that lies between two rock outcrops in the Tofana, to Col Drusciè, the first section of the "Freccia nel Cielo" Cableway. It is a slope for experts which includes three jumps, one of which is oriented completely towards Cortina.

The slope descending from Monte Lagazuoi (photo 211) is always sunlit and is a strip that unwinds in a sea of rocks. The Cinque Torri seem to guard the beautiful slope bearing the same name (photo 217) and unwinding in the woods in a series of wide curves and little jumps that make it extremely varying. As it is exposed northwards, the snow here is practically guaranteed at all times and the vast array of slopes make it pleasant to sportsmen of all levels.

211 CORTINA CERTAINLY OFFERS THE MOST SPECTACULAR SLOPES IN THE WORLD!

For those who love cross country skiing, what is known as nordic skiing in Olympic races, there is nothing better than a track along an apparently levelled plane in the woods. At Fiames, the cross country ring has many variants permitting skiers to choose a longer track according to their will.

Cross country skiers shun all technological innovations and love to slide on the snow, as if strolling in the mountains.

What better setting than Lake Landro with one flank covered with trees reaching right down to its frozen surface?

The track that runs along the old railway, too, is perfect for lovers of this winter sport and, in the summer, it becomes a pleasant trail to ride down on a mountain bike. It is also the Dobbiaco-Cortina track, the famous race open to all, though it is an international race.

212 STARTING TIME OF THE "DOBBIACO-CORTINA".

213 CROSS COUNTRY SKIING TRACKS.

214 MOUNT FALORIA IN THE SHARP SUNSET LIGHT.

Those who prefer less hard work and looking-on, have numerous opportunities for doing simply this. For example, many dog-sled races are held and one can admire the dogs running fast through the woods pulling their sleds and "Mushers". Participants come from Canada, Alaska and many European countries to race all over the Alps and down to Cortina. After a hectic start, the track is followed in silence, as every ounce of energy must be used for the race alone.

216 Dog-sled race.

217 The Cinque Torri ski slope.

215 Acrobatic skiing.

Bobsleighing reached Cortina at the beginning of 1900 and precisely in 1906. At that time there was no track and these very fast "sleighs" ran along the Dolomites road, between Pocol and Cortina. In 1923 the construction of an actual track began and this was updated on the occasion of the 1956 Olympic Games.

Today it measures 1300 meters in length, with 11 spectacular and blood-chilling curves. Training after training, for a race that lasts merely 55 seconds, but where emotions are great.

The Cortina Hockey team, founded in 1924, experienced brighter days than those of the past few years. The current team - called "Sportivi Ghiaccio Cortina" - has already won 14 championships, the first being in 1932.

218 DESCENT DOWN THE OLYMPIC BOBSLEIGH TRACK.

220 ICE HOCKEY MATCH.

219 STARTING OF A FOUR-MAN BOBSLEIGH RACE.

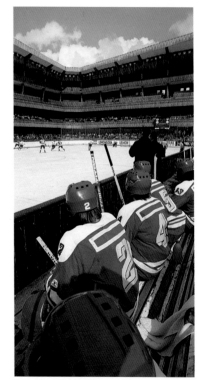

221 THE OLYMPIC STADIUM.

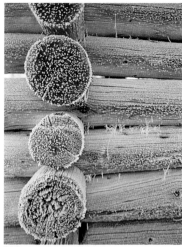

One may think it funny that all winter sports entail speed or, at least, competition.
However, Cortina also holds a more intimate aspect which goes beyond society life and sporting activities that always entail moving frenzy. The quiet aspect of Cortina is that which perhaps everyone remembers when leaving Cortina itself. It is not the shops, slopes or elegant restaurants that remain impressed in our memories; it is the feeling of intimate heat warming up the hearts of those who love Cortina and wish to understand her profoundly.

222 THE BOROUGH OF COL.

223 A FROZEN ALPINE HUT.

224 A FARM-HOUSE AFTER A SNOWFALL.

225 TYPICAL AMPEZZO WOODEN ARCHITECTURE.

PHOTO BY LUCIANA ZARDINI

Stefano Zardini was born in Cortina of a family of photographers. Already in 1890 his grandfather Raffaele ran a photographic laboratory and studio in the town. Since then, the Zardini family has continued to document, for over a century, the history and everyday life of Cortina, until the setting up of their renown shop in Corso Italia, which is still today a reference point to all photography-lovers. Today, at its third generation, Stefano Zardini continues this work expanding his interest to cover far away Countries. On behalf of the League of Red Cross Societies, he crossed the entire southern Sahara to document the great drought that hit the Sahel region.

He continued his reportages on South African mines, gorillas, the Virunga volcanos, on the civil wars waging in Mozambique and in Angola. He was then sent to the Middle East to report on the Iran-Iraq war, on Kuwait, Oman and other Arab Countries. He also did other reportages in Northern Vietnam, Ladak and Nepal. His works are published in some of the most distinguished international magazines. In Italy he collaborates with Airone, Atlante, Panorama, A.D. Bell'Italia, and "7" of the "Corriere della Sera". among his published works are "Rottweiler" for Mursia, "Cortina d'Ampezzo" with M.F. Belli, "Almerindo" and "Delicatessen" with Giorgio Soavi and varoius volumes with Mariapia Fanfani. He is also the author of various films: in the world of sports (Marlboro Pirelli Award); in the world of alpinism (Festival of Trento Award); in the humanitarian field (Armenia and Bangladesh) and for a number of important industrial groups: Barilla, Agroalimentare, ICI Pharma, etc.. One of his filmed strips on the problem of hunger in Africa was shown at the United Nations. Stefano Zardini still works as a reporter.